If you've ever wanted to build something that truly matters, beyond profit or recognition, this book is your guide. Dan's wisdom runs deep, but it's his humanity that makes his message unforgettable.
Alex Melen | Co-Founder, SmartSites

No Ego Policy is more than a book. It's a movement toward workplaces that value love, laughter, and authenticity as much as performance and results.
Shawn Johal | Business Growth Coach, Elevation Leaders, Bestselling Author of *The Happy Leader*

Dan doesn't tell you how to lead; he shows you what it looks like when it's done right. His stories stay with you long after the last page.
Casel Burnett | Vice President, LODI, and International Bestselling Author of *No Regrets*

Every company says "culture matters," but few explain how to build one that lasts. Dan does it with heart, humor, and real-world experience that makes it all feel possible.
Bryan Howard | CEO of Peoplyst, Author of *The Vanguard Edge*

No EGO Policy isn't just a leadership book it's a reminder of what truly matters. Daniel Batty writes with a rare honesty, humility, and heart that you can feel on every page. His stories from construction sites to corporate boardrooms to the quiet, sacred moments of real human connection show that culture isn't a strategy; it's a way of life.

Daniel takes you into the trenches of leadership and shows you what it looks like to serve with love, lead with conviction, and build something that outlives you. This book is a masterclass in building teams, lifting people, and creating environments where others can grow into who they were meant to become.

For anyone who wants to build a company with soul... for any leader who believes people come before process for anyone who has ever wondered whether love still has a place in business this book is your answer.

Daniel doesn't just teach culture he lives it. And after reading this book, you'll want to do the same.
Anthony Amunategui | Founder, CDO Group

Unlike most books I have read about business and business culture, *No Ego Policy* resonated more deeply with me primarily because of Dan's insightful mantra about leading with love, laughter and authenticity.
Myles Mordaunt | Owner, Icon Property Group of Companies - Monaco

Dan has written a book that reminds leaders what truly matters. *No Ego Policy* pulls you in with raw stories, honest lessons, and a call to lead with heart. It made me reflect on my own leadership journey and rethink the small moments that shape culture. This isn't theory. It's lived experience, and it shows.
Andrew K. Smith | Managing Director & Cofounder, Savory Fund

No Ego Policy

Culture Reimagined: Leading
with Love and Authenticity

Leaders
Press

DANIEL J. BATTY

Table of Contents

Foreword

When I think about leaders who truly "get" culture, Daniel Batty is one of the first names that comes to mind. I've had the privilege of working alongside Daniel for several years, as my company, Main & Main, partnered with Dutch Bros on its nationwide expansion. The pace of growth could have been overwhelming, but even in the busiest, highest-pressure moments, Daniel led with calm, kindness, and clarity– to the way he worked with his team, vendors, and partners.

What I respect most about Daniel is his ability to make culture practical. He isn't just a builder of stores; he's a builder of trust and of people. Rather than speak in lofty abstractions, he shows you how to shape culture, measure it, and protect it. Just as importantly, he brings people together, aligning operations and partnerships through processes that not only deliver results but also strengthen culture at every step. That's precisely what you'll find in the pages: insights from someone who has led through the pressures of rapid growth while never losing sight of the people who make it possible.

If you're picking up this book, you already know culture matters. What Daniel offers is a clear and actionable guide to putting that belief into practice. He'll challenge assumptions, share stories you won't forget, and provide lessons you can apply right away.

I can't think of a better person to lead this conversation. Daniel has lived what he teaches, and his leadership proves that when you prioritize people, culture, and consistency, you don't just grow a business, you build something that lasts.

Garrett Reed CEO
Layne's Chicken Fingers
Founder, Main + Main

Garrett Reed is the CEO and co-owner of Layne's Chicken Fingers, the fast-casual restaurant concept founded in 1994 in College Station, Texas. Since acquiring the brand in 2017 from longtime owner Mike Garratt, he has led its evolution from a regional favorite into a disciplined, growth-focused franchise. Drawing on a successful background in commercial real estate and development—including roles in site selection, real estate leadership for major tenants, and his own development firm—Reed brings both operational expertise and a people-first philosophy to his work. He emphasizes culture, quality, and team development alongside reliable systems and strong vendor partnerships, ensuring Layne's remains true to its roots while scaling. Under his leadership, the brand has grown to more than 25 locations with ambitious plans for continued expansion nationwide.

Preface

"Kindness is the language which the deaf can hear and the blind can see."

—Mark Twain

Welcome to the beginning of something different.

This book begins in a single moment, a Wednesday morning, standing in my parents' garage. Every leader has one: when momentum turns to silence, and the chase for more gives way to the ache for meaning.

The experience of that day hasn't slowed me down; it has driven me harder, with a clearer vision and more profound conviction. Now that the fog has lifted, what remains has become the heartbeat of leadership: to love the people I work alongside and to build cultures that do the same.

Over the years, titles, success, and ambition have started to feel insignificant. I've realized that leadership isn't about building empires; it's about serving others and leaving the world better than you found it.

I stopped measuring success by how much our team grew a brand and started focusing on how we built it, and who we became along the way. That shift in my thinking has led to stronger teams, happier employees, and accelerated growth. It reminded me of something business rarely talks about but always proves true: love wins.

Love might not be the first word you expect to find in a business book, but it should be. I grew up in a faith-driven home, and although that influenced many of my values, the principle of love guides how I've led throughout my career.

And before you roll your eyes and dismiss that as idealistic fluff, let me assure you, love works. Compassion builds trust, and genuine care invites innovation. When people feel deeply valued, they want to show up, stay late, and give their best. People are loyal to leaders who care and for a culture that turns work into purpose.

This book is for the CEO trying to reconnect with their team, and the first-time manager deciding whether to emulate their boss or become the leader they always wished they had. It's for the barista, the construction foreman, the front-desk receptionist, or anyone who believes work should be more than survival. Work should be where we live out our purpose and inspire the people we serve as leaders.

Throughout my career, I've believed you don't need to intimidate or micromanage people to get them to strive for success, be motivated, or execute at a high level. "Love is All You Need" (*to be so bold as to borrow from the Beatles*). That belief hasn't always aligned with the leadership styles I've encountered, but time and again, I've seen the golden rule prove itself in business as in life: treat others the way you want to be treated.

Look at some of the most successful companies in the world: Google, Chick-fil-A, Patagonia, Dutch Bros Coffee, REI, Savory Brands and Zappos. They've embraced the idea of a People First mindset, purpose-driven values, and a commitment to bettering the world around them. Leading with love works. It boosts retention, increases productivity, and fosters innovation through more creative and inclusive thinking.

When people believe in the culture, they give their all. They work harder, remain longer, and live happier lives. That's what this book is about. Whether you're a corporate executive or a college student, I hope you'll find something in these pages to help you lead better, love deeper, and build a culture worth fighting for.

But let's be clear: culture doesn't build itself; it defaults. And when it defaults, it can drift toward fear, selfishness, confusion, or burnout. Without intentional care, the wrong seeds grow. This book is a guide to help you choose those seeds wisely and cultivate a culture worth belonging to.

That's why I call this the *No EGO Policy*. Years ago, in a conversation with Pastor Mike Carlisle, he told me, "Dan, EGO stands for *Edging God Out*." He reminded me that the moment we start believing we're bigger than the plan, more important than the people around us, or act as if we're untouchable or unaccountable, that's when life humbles us. That conversation stuck with me, and over time, it evolved into my guiding mantra: operate with a *No EGO Policy*.

To me, that means choosing humility over hierarchy, collaboration over control, and:

- Committing to a shared mission over individual credit.
- Welcoming respectful pushback and diverse perspectives.
- Honoring the "expert in the room," no matter their title.
- Pausing after big milestones to celebrate, reflect, and grow.
- Practicing what I call *Love and Lift*, seeing each other, supporting each other, and never missing the chance to speak life into the people beside us.

This isn't theory. It's the way I've led construction crews, restaurant teams, and corporate divisions. It works at places like Dutch Bros and Trader Joe's, and it's what I've experienced during seasons of tragedy, burnout, and renewal.

If you've spent any time with me, you've likely been bombarded by quips that may or may not make immediate sense until you understand the context:

- "Fair, Firm & Friendly"
- LOVE means: "Laugh Often, Value Everyone"
- "When it's odd, it's God."
- And, of course, the inspiration for this book: "No EGO Policy"

These are simple ideas that hold a lifetime of lessons, faith, and experiences behind them. Each one reflects a different way of seeing leadership through love, and together, they form the rhythm that has guided my life and career.

In the chapters ahead, you'll find stories from the trenches—some inspiring, some painful, all honest. You'll see lessons from businesses that got it right, and from those that didn't. Along the way, you'll find tools you can use, encouragement when you need it, and more than a few laughs. Because if we're not laughing, we're probably not loving each other very well either.

This isn't a book of theories; it's a book of real stories told through experience. Some of them mine, some of them yours, but all of them point to the same truth: when we choose to serve others, culture doesn't just change; it transforms.

Culture is the lifeblood of your business. It's the vibe, the heartbeat, the glue. Get it right, and you'll create a great place to work while building a legacy that people may never forget.

So, let's start here, together:

"In this place, we do things differently. We lead with love."

CHAPTER 1

The Power of Story

"The story you often get is not the story you were chasing, but it ends up being even better."

–Anthony Bourdain

Backstage Leadership: Presence over Position

Attending a Marc Anthony concert was more than just entertainment; it was a masterclass in leadership. With the lights, the music, and the energy, Marc poured his soul into every note like only he could. But the moment that impacted me didn't happen onstage. It happened in the shadows, quiet, powerful, and easy to miss if you weren't paying attention, but something I couldn't stop thinking about.

Before the show, I watched Gus Zambrano, Marc's head of global security, walk into the arena with calm, unshakable authority. Gus isn't just known for protecting world-class talent; he's known for building world-class teams. And on this night, that reputation was on full display. The Toyota Arena hired the team that evening, and it was not part of Marc Anthony's typical security detail, but Gus changed that perception in an instant. One by one, he approached each member of the security team at the venue. There was no fanfare or overreach. Just Gus, who made direct eye contact, extended his hand for a firm handshake, and gave a sincere "thank you" to each person on staff who was there that evening.

Watching this unfold, something remarkable happened. Every person he engaged with just lit up. You could see it in their posture, which changed after Gus extended his special brand of culture into the venue. Their focus sharpened, and their demeanor shifted. In that instance, they became part of something bigger, 'protectors of the experience.'

If anything had gone wrong that night, those individuals would've responded with everything they had. Not because they were told to, but because someone made them feel seen and essential to the experience. That's the power of creating a strong culture. Sometimes it shows up as a handshake: a quiet moment, or a leader who understands that presence is more powerful than position.

Gus doesn't just protect Marc Anthony; he protects the atmosphere. That night, the culture came alive with the crowd, the incredible music, and Marc commanding the stage. It was a fantastic evening, but it was defined by how the team responded to a person who laid the foundation for protection and demonstrated humility in serving others. That's what true culture looks like. It's built on the small, meaningful moments between people. Culture is lived, not scripted. That same truth also applies to storytelling.

The Story Defines the Journey

Have you ever been halfway through a project and suddenly thought, 'Wait. . .why are we doing this again?'

If so, you're not alone.

"Why" is a defining question in business, leadership, and life. It's the backbone of everything that matters. Without a clear why, even bold strategies lose their spark, and the best-intended teams start to drift. It's like running a steakhouse that serves tofu: you may offer excellent service, but the message is misaligned and ultimately forgettable.

When the "Why" is clear, something shifts. Culture comes alive, decisions snap into focus, and the experience inspires your team. They will start to believe in what's being built and will want to be a part of it. In Simon Sinek's book, *Start with Why*, he states that the "Why" is the fundamental core of business, and it's the foundation upon which "How" and "What" are built[1].

For Dutch Bros, their goal wasn't to be the largest coffee chain. It was simpler and more powerful: *to make a massive difference, one cup at a time.* For the people at the brand, this purpose goes beyond serving coffee; it's about creating genuine human connections and uplifting communities. As their founder often states, "We may sell coffee, but we're in the relationship business." That mission adds meaning to every interaction, from a Broista spending an extra minute talking about a customer's dog, asking about family, or celebrating a win. These aren't just transactions, they're connections.

When people ask what makes the culture thrive, tell them it starts with a true story. Not the carefully worded "About Us" on a website, but the raw, honest story about the risks, the vision, the stumbles, and the heart that sparked the business in the first place.

---

[1] Sinek, Simon. Start with Why: How Great Leaders Inspire Everyone to Take Action. Portfolio, 2009.

Belief in your brand and vision doesn't happen by accident; it's built through the clarity that connects a business and its customers around a shared purpose. That clarity takes root in something deeper: a story of identity and intent. Every business begins somewhere, and at its core is a heartbeat that sets the direction for everything that follows.

Even before my time with Dutch Bros, I had worked in construction and land development. It is gritty, deadline-driven work where weather, inspectors, and budgets don't care about intentions. No one dared speak of culture on a jobsite, or you might have been chased off. But I learned that people profoundly shape culture, whether they name it or not. One person or group sets the tone, making the culture better, or breaking it. The best way to lead, inspire, and align wasn't through policies; it was through creating buy-in and purpose. And what is the best way to express that purpose? Through a story.

At the time, I didn't think of it as storytelling. I just knew that if I couldn't explain why something mattered, whether to a city planner, an investor, or a laborer on the brink of burnout, things fell apart. But when I could connect the task to something more profound, when I could show how it all fit into a bigger picture, people leaned in and bought into the story we were selling.

A good story builds trust and shows vulnerability. It creates a connection that says, "I've been through something, and here's what I've learned." And that's the beginning of how real culture starts to form.

Trash Talk & Truths

For a short but wildly entertaining season, I worked for SOLAG Disposal, a waste hauling firm in South Orange County, California. The CEO, Tom Trulis, was part boss, part stand-up comic. He could turn a room of serious people into a laugh track. Underneath the wit was a sharp operator who under-stood human nature. In five years together, he must've rattled off 200 jokes—never the same one twice. When we golfed, he'd remind me I was the worst golfer he'd seen, but said the laughter we shared together made it worthwhile.

One moment in particular made an indelible impression on me. We were meeting with a local jurisdiction to discuss a potential rate increase for trash hauling, and the City was pushing back strongly. It was frustrating for everyone at the table. Competition at the time was fierce, and we could not afford to lose the contract. Costs across the industry were ris-ing—wages, gas, equipment—yet the City's responsibility was to act in the best interest of its citizens. We were at a standstill, and the tension in the room was thick.

In the middle of the back-and-forth, Tom paused. He shifted the conversation with a story. I can't recall all the details, but I remember how the atmosphere changed. He began talking about his family's emigration from Greece and the challenges he faced growing up, including learning a new language, adjusting to a new culture, and struggling to find his place in it. It was deeply personal and completely unexpected.

As he spoke, the room softened. People leaned back in their chairs, the tension eased, and for a moment, it felt less like a negotiation and more like a conversation. Somehow, Tom tied his story back to why we were all sitting at that table, and it was nothing short of magical. It wasn't about increasing costs any-more; it was about shared humanity and the universal struggle to find a sense of belonging. I was utterly drawn in, and I had almost forgotten we were there to negotiate a rate increase.

And yet, somehow, we walked out of that meeting with an addendum to the contract, and the rate increase was approved with no hard sell or arm-twisting. Just a heartfelt story that cuts through the noise.

That moment has stuck with me ever since. It was a masterclass in what truly moves people; it's a genuine connection. Stories disarm people; they can build a relationship and remind people there's a human on the other side of the table.

That day, in a room full of city officials and trash talk (the clean kind), Tom didn't just negotiate a contract; he built a bridge. And in the messy world of hauling garbage, that was pure gold.

The Role of Authenticity in Storytelling

Let's be real: people can sniff out fake from a mile away. Especially today, when both employees and customers are more discerning, skeptical, and value-driven than ever before. If your story feels too polished, too perfect, or too rehearsed, it won't land. And worse, it could backfire.

When we ask leaders about their why, we're looking for the truth beneath the surface: what drives them, what nearly broke them, and what keeps them coming back. The real questions are: Why does your company exist? What kept you going in the early days? Who believed in you when they had nothing to gain? What moment nearly made you call it quits, and what made you get back up after you were knocked down?

Authenticity doesn't mean you have it all figured out. It means you're honest about the mess, and you've found meaning in it. That's why, of all the roles throughout my career, Dutch Bros stood out for how they navigated the work environment. Their founders didn't start with a five-year business plan, but with a pushcart, a big dream, and even bigger hearts. They told their story from the very beginning, and more importantly, they lived it. Every employee knows the growth, and every customer feels it.

When I joined the team, I didn't just adopt the brand; I became part of the story. They trusted me to carry the heartbeat forward, to help write the next chapter. This is what the best organizations create: they expand the story, make room for new characters, and they keep the original heartbeat pulsing through every decision.

Today, that kind of authenticity doesn't need to be confined within the walls of the organization or your current customer base. With the advent of social media, every brand has the opportunity to share its story, competing on a level playing field with its larger competitors. It doesn't take extravagant budgets to reach your customers; it takes a story people believe in, amplified through the channels now at everyone's fingertips.

Why This Matters Now More than Ever

The world has changed. And with it, so have people's expectations. We're living in a time when employees aren't just looking for a paycheck or security; they're searching for significance. They want to know that their work matters, that they belong to something bigger, and that their effort is building something meaningful. In this post-pandemic, digitally disconnected, fast-changing world, culture isn't a luxury; it's oxygen. And the story you tell—the story you live—is the breath that keeps your people going. Your team doesn't just want to know what to do or how to do it. They want to know why it matters. They want to know who they're doing it with, and they want to believe that it counts for something.

So, tell them. Start at the very beginning and tell them the origin story, about the win that lit the fire and the failure that almost put it out. Tell them what you've learned along the way, what you still believe in, and the reason this business is worth showing up for each day. Because when people hear your why and they believe it's real, they'll carry the torch for you. That's how culture grows, teams endure, and how legacies are built.

CHAPTER 2

Built from the Ground Up

"A society grows great when old men plant trees in whose shade they shall never sit."

—Greek Proverb

The Last Big Set: Perfect Waves, the Wipeout, and the Promise

High school was chaos. It was a wild mix of surfing, skateboarding, beach parties, and, if we're being honest, skipping class. I tried out for sports but never stuck with any of them. Football meant missing the best summer swells. Tennis took me away from skating local pools and "gunning" the once-famous Churchill. Track? Forget it. Team sports bored me. I could hold my own, but the ocean and adventure always won.

If you grew up in San Clemente in the late '70s or early '80s, you know I wasn't alone. The town was crawling with future legends: Matt Archibald, Dino Andino, Shane Beschen, Brian McNulty, Jimmy Hogan, Jorga and Jolene Smith, the Paskowitz crew—kids who would later make names for themselves in surf history. We'd spot a young Kelly Slater or others chasing the Trestles dream, paddling out at Lowers or Cottons, or other surf spots around town (204, Lowers, Old Mans, Poche, Cottons, Churches, T-Street, San Clemente Pier, and others), hoping to steal a wave or two.

Our surfboards were shaped by local legends like Hobie Alter, Herbie Fletcher, Danny Brawner, Midget Smith, Rick James, Phil Edwards, Dewey Weber, and many others. It was the golden age of grit and fiberglass, and an epic time to grow up in my hometown. Surfing is the heartbeat of our town.

One winter in '83, my brother and I paddled out into a monster swell—fifteen-foot faces and a ripping current that turned the water into a washing machine. Our dad stood on the shore, hands in his pockets, praying silently that we'd make it back in one piece. Later, he told us he realized in that moment he couldn't get us anymore. We were on our own.

I still remember the sound of those waves, how they roared and hissed like a living thing. At one point, I got caught inside and was held under for what felt like forever. Everything went black. Then, just when I thought I was out of air, I shot to the surface and grabbed one breath before getting slammed underneath the surface again. Somehow, I always managed to come up, always found the shore, and was able to make it home.

At the time, I didn't realize that day would become one of the greatest metaphors for leadership and life I'd ever experience.

You see, leadership isn't about controlling the waves; it's about learning to ride them. The ocean doesn't care about your ego, your title, or your perfect plan. It humbles you, teaches you rhythm, and demands you pay attention. It rewards those who respect its power and punishes those who pretend to own it.

Culture works the same way. You can't muscle your way through it. You have to feel it, read the currents, trust your instincts, and paddle out even when it looks terrifying. You'll wipe out, get tumbled, lose your breath, and want to quit. But if you keep showing up, with love, humility, and courage, the ocean will eventually embrace you.

That day, I learned something I've carried ever since:

You can't lead from the shore. You have to paddle out.

And sometimes, the biggest waves reveal the kind of leader–and human–you were meant to be.

The ocean taught me to lead without control. My father taught me to love without condition.
Those lessons came long before business, before titles, before I knew what "culture" even meant. They began in a dusty Los Angeles truck called Rusty Buckets, on a jobsite where I learned that leadership starts at home.

The Impact of Friends and Family: Some Real, Some Imagined

> *"My father didn't tell me how to live; he lived and let me watch him do it."*
>
> —Clarence Budington Kelland

The first time I felt part of something bigger was on a jobsite with my dad. I was eight, riding shotgun in his beat-up truck "Rusty Buckets," bouncing down dusty streets in Los Angeles. We pulled up to a site, and he handed me a tape measure. "Hold the end of this."

For thirty minutes, we worked together measuring electrical runs. He had done the same thing the day before, but something didn't feel right. He needed a second set of hands, and I was proud to be the one to help. When we finished, he wrapped me in a big hug. "You just saved my ass," he said, laughing. "I really needed your help today."

My reward was breakfast with my father. We celebrated at Penny's Diner in Los Angeles—think Denny's, but with pennies sealed in resin across the countertop. It was one of my favorite places and is forever etched in my memory as sacred ground. That breakfast was one of my earliest experiences of working, and the reward of a 'job well done' filled me with a sense of accomplishment. More than the pancakes, it was the quiet joy of being needed, appreciated, and trusted.

Lessons like that didn't happen in isolation; my environment helped to shape them. Growing up in a working-class family in La Crescenta, California, meant living in a neighborhood where steady values met remarkable people with extraordinary stories. Life there wasn't glamorous, but it was rich in character. Sundays meant attending St. James the Less Catholic Church, where faith anchored our family and community. We camped often, spent weekends with friends, and we all showed up for each other through thick and thin. My parents ensured that we were present, respectful, grounded, and well-dressed. Our home was always open, a revolving door of friends and family who shared in our struggles and celebrated our victories. It was a place of laughter, resilience, and quiet lessons in what it meant to belong.

Perhaps the most influential relationship my parents had was with the Rohan family. There were five brothers who all worked together in the family's HVAC business. We were the closest with Uncle John and Aunt Sally (not real family, but they should have been). The Rohans had built a family compound just up the street from our home. The brothers lived side by side on the same street, and their mother had the largest house at the end of the block. It was situated so that the yard and pool were designed to let her share in the grandchildren's childhood moments and be present at countless family gatherings. For our family, it felt like having a front-row seat to something extraordinary.

The Rohan clan carried an ease about them, full of warmth and love, shaping a life grounded in devotion, loyalty, and generosity. Everything they did seemed designed to strengthen one another and to pass down a spirit of connection from one generation to the next. Guided by the wisdom of their parents, their choices were intentional, preserving unity, deepening legacy, and building a foundation for prosperity that stretched beyond material wealth. Watching them taught me that true success wasn't measured by status or money, but by the strength of relationships and the love you leave behind.

Others also left a lasting mark. Men whose presence quietly shaped my understanding of leadership, success, and grace. One of those men was someone my brother and I called "Mr. Brown from China." He was the first person I ever met who traveled internationally, and to a young, idealistic kid dreaming of faraway places, he felt larger than life. China just happened to be where he was headed next, but to us, he might as well have been an explorer charting new worlds. Then there was Mr. Cameron, a polished Vice President for Monroe Shocks, who looked like he'd stepped straight out of *Mad Men*; sophisticated, handsome, perfectly dressed, articulate, and never without a scotch in hand after five o'clock. He carried himself with effortless confidence, making business seem like an art form and commanding respect through his presence alone. He'd often bring us stacks of Monroe Shock stickers—something small, but to a young boy, it made him unforgettable. And up the street lived a Standard Oil worker whose success was secured through stock options that changed his family's life forever. That stroke of fortune taught me what can happen when discipline, timing, and opportunity finally align. It took me years to understand what this meant, but even then, I sensed the quiet power of preparation meeting possibility.

It wasn't just their success that stayed with me; it was how they carried themselves. Each of these men possessed a quiet strength, a sense of purpose, and a dignity that seemed to fill a room without saying much to me at all. They came and went from our home often, their laughter and conversation bringing warmth and energy that lingered long after they left. Without realizing it, each man left something behind: a spark of inspiration, a piece of wisdom, a glimpse of what leadership looked like when paired with humility. Looking back, I now see how those encounters planted the early seeds of curiosity and ambition, along with the understanding that a meaningful life isn't built solely on accomplishments, but on character and substance.

Our family spent much of our time with these families, including the Rohans, Pfeifles, and Crezcenzi. Most of these relationships were made at church, and my father seemed to navigate towards men who shared the same values (including his golfing and drinking abilities). Our homes were filled with joy, the occasional prank, and plenty of Sunday morning brunches. Though all of these men came from different backgrounds and walks of life, what bound them together was a shared commitment to their families.

These men weren't just names or neighbors; they were bound together by loyalty and shared purpose, facing life's struggles like brothers in arms. Through them, and thanks to my mom and dad, I learned what it means to build and maintain relationships rooted in sacrifice, trust, and hard work. None of them were superheroes; they were ordinary men who worked tirelessly, took risks, and built meaningful lives from the ground up. Yet their ordinary lives left extraordinary marks. Each of these local legends, from different corners of the community, became quiet role models—men my parents admired and learned from, who taught through example more than with words. What I didn't realize then was how deeply those everyday interactions were shaping my definition of success. Even now, decades later, many of those same family connections remain—and I'm grateful every day for the foundation our parents built together.

I didn't know it then, but those early lessons in humility and leadership would come rushing back years later. At the same time, golfing in California would leave me forever changed, reshaping how I understood influence, presence, and connection.

The Comedian and Politician

At about eight or nine, our family was vacationing in Palm Springs, CA, when my dad decided to take my brother and me golfing. We were hitting balls at the practice range—slicing, hooking, tearing up the grass. My father had positioned us at the far end so we wouldn't disturb the other golfers when a man approached. I thought we were in trouble and would be removed from the driving range. Instead, he walked over, introduced himself to us, shook our hands, and chatted with my dad as if he were an old friend.

As we walked to the car, I asked, "Dad, is that someone you work with?"

That stopped my father dead in his tracks. "What? That was Bob Hope! Don't you know who Bob Hope is?"

I didn't know then, Dad, but I promise you I do now. . .Wow!

Bob Hope wasn't just a celebrity; he was a global icon who made the world laugh for decades—known for his quick wit, tireless energy, and over seventy films, including the *Road to. . .* series with Bing Crosby. He became a fixture of American entertainment. Offstage, he was just as extraordinary, devoting himself to entertaining U.S. troops on nearly sixty tours from World War II through the Gulf War. His real gift wasn't just comedy; it was connection. He had a way of making everyone feel seen, even two wide-eyed kids on a driving range with their dad.

That wouldn't be the last time I crossed paths with someone whose influence reached far beyond my world. A few years later, another chance encounter left just as deep a mark, this time not with an entertainer but with a former President.

In 1974, our family began a new chapter, moving to San Clemente, CA, a quiet surf town with fewer than 17,000 residents (it has since grown to nearly 70,000 today). There, I became a wild California kid: surfing, riding motorcycles, and hustling golf balls at Shorecliffs Golf Course. That's where I met President Nixon.

Yes, President Richard Nixon.

He lived in San Clemente, in a place famously known as the Western White House, and he often played golf at Shorecliffs Golf Club. Many afternoons after school, I would set up shop by the 16th hole with egg cartons full of "experienced" golf balls that were hunted down days earlier in the brush. I was proud of my business and would wash and clean the golf balls before presenting them for sale. I usually spotted his

Secret Service detail before he arrived, and soon enough, we became familiar faces to one another. When his "motorcade" stopped, the ritual was always the same.

"Hello, Danny," he'd say with a smile.

The agents knew me by name and would inspect my collection first before the President picked out a few. Over time, our small exchanges evolved into something that felt like a genuine friendship. President Nixon introduced me to astronauts, politicians, and once, Vice President Spiro Agnew, who handed me a golf ball with his face printed on it, a treasure to a kid who idolized anyone of this stature.

One afternoon, Nixon reached into his pocket and said, "Two bits for a golf ball?"
Confused, I replied, "They're twenty-five cents, Mr. President."
He laughed and explained that "two bits" *meant* a quarter—one-eighth of a dollar. From then on, it became our running joke. Whenever he approached the tee, I'd call out, "Golf balls, two bits!" and he'd grin like we shared a secret.

A year or so into my friendship with the President, I was telling my Aunt Dot (*Dorothy Crezcenzi, not a real aunt, but part of our extended family*) about how I regularly saw Richard Nixon playing golf. She was at our home a few weeks later when I noticed his security detail rounding the 15th hole, and I pointed him out to her. She beamed with excitement and asked, "Can you get me his autograph, Danny? He is my favorite President!" I ran down our back hill, confident my friend would oblige. "Mr. President, can I get your autograph for my Aunt Dot?"

"Aunt Dot?" he asked, smiling. "Is her name Dorothy?"

I paused and thought about that question. "I don't know," I said. "She's just Aunt Dot!"

He laughed and signed, "To Aunt Dot, Love Richard Nixon." That autograph stayed framed in her home until the day she passed, a simple gesture by a former President that became a memorable keepsake.

Those moments made me feel important. I was a young, eager kid who probably seemed like a pest to the surrounding adults, yet they always gave me their time. From them, I learned the value of truly 'seeing' people. That simple act of kindness from Bob Hope, and later from President Nixon, left a lasting impression on me: a reminder that even the smallest gestures can have the deepest impact.

Memories of My Father

My father spent almost his entire life in construction, coming home tired, dirty, and beat up from long days in the field. Every callus, bruise, and blister was a reminder of the hard, physical, and dangerous work he did to support our family. If you've ever had a family member in construction, you know the pride and how every street held a story. We couldn't drive anywhere without my father pointing out the projects he had worked on (I have that same affliction, which my kids call 'construction tour-guide syndrome'). I was proud of my father. He didn't just build structures; he built a life far removed from the tough childhood he came from, and he carried that pride with him every mile.

Having grown up extremely poor and under challenging circumstances, he left home at fourteen, later serving in the Korean War, and eventually returned, determined to improve his life. He quickly sought out my mom, whom he had met in high school, and had an on-again/off-again relationship. They rekindled that spark and were soon married. At the time, my mother was a receptionist for a contractor, and she helped get him an interview to join his business as an apprentice electrician. Eventually, he earned his contractor's license, which led us to San Clemente. My parents provided us with a good life, not in terms of financial wealth, but one overflowing with love.

Throughout my lifetime, I watched my father interact with people and noticed that he respected everyone. There was never a time I saw my father turn his back on anyone in need. He gladly served members of the immigrant community, business owners who would trade work for goods or services when they couldn't afford his fees, and he was one of the few contractors willing to work in the homosexual community of Laguna Beach. He had friends from every walk of life, rich, poor, young, and old, immigrants, business owners, and even a transgender woman from our neighboring community. Having grown up under challenging circumstances, he was street-smart but also understood people's struggles on a personal level. Because of this, he could talk to anyone, and people enjoyed his company. He had strong discipline, and his words carried weight and although he had a tough exterior, he always led with love. Always.

Those early lessons became the blueprint for everything that followed.

My Own Story

From a young age, I knew I wasn't destined to follow my father's path and strap on a toolbelt. I was chasing something different, something bigger. I dreamed of being a police officer, another day a soldier, an actor, a stuntman, or even a rodeo clown. Whatever path I chose, I was determined to give it everything it required.

Still, there was something incredible about watching my dad in his element, managing a crew, and navigating a job site like a general on the battlefield. He was calm under pressure, sharp with humor, friendly with everyone, and precise in his execution. A war veteran raised in harsh conditions, he was tough as nails but earned respect through grace and grit. People who worked alongside him never hesitated to pull my brothers and me aside to say, "Your dad is one of the best." And every time, I stood a little taller when I got to answer, "Yeah… he's my dad."

Work ethic was gospel in our home—no questions, no exceptions. It wasn't something we discussed often; it was simply understood. At age 12, I delivered papers for *The Daily Sun Post*, carefully folding each one into aerodynamic torpedoes and launching them with precision. If one landed in a puddle, or the customer couldn't locate the paper? There were no excuses. I would have to ride my bicycle back to the customer and replace the newspaper *(or find wherever I had thrown it)*. By 14, I was well on my way to success, washing dishes at a Chinese restaurant for $1.75 an hour, my hands pruning in soapy water while the cooks barked orders in Cantonese, the steam fogging up the room, and sweat soaking my clothes.

Then came the Ocean View Tennis Club. I must have done a great job washing dishes, because soon I was washing down tennis courts. Over time, I began stringing rackets, giving lessons, playing matches, and eventually working my way up to assistant manager. I made the most of my time in that clubhouse under the guidance of an incredible leader, Alex Ott. While the other kids were playing on the courts, I would sit inside the clubhouse, listening to stories and talking with adults about their careers, their successes, their failures, and what it truly took to make something of themselves. I didn't want shortcuts; I wanted a road map and the hope that someone would take me under their wing. It never happened *(not in the way I wanted, but let's save that for my next book)*.

And through it all, I continued to work for my dad. On weekends, summer breaks, holidays—you name it. Whether it was helping him with concrete forms, digging ditches, pulling wire, or holding a flashlight while he worked late into the night, I stayed close to the trades, and it kept me grounded.

I understood the risks and hard work of my father's business, but nothing could prepare me for the moment when it almost claimed my brother's life.

The instance that solidified the fact that I would never follow my father's path came the day my older brother, Mike, got electrocuted while working on a junction box from the top of a twenty-five-foot ladder. It was an oversight that would turn a routine task into a near-deadly experience when the circuit hadn't been fully de-energized. The moment Mike's hand touched the wires, the current locked him in place and sent a violent jolt through his body. His arms seized, his whole frame convulsed, and he was trapped, frozen in midair by raw electricity.

My dad, working nearby, saw what was happening and sprinted to the base of the ladder. Scrambling up with the urgency only a parent knows, shouting Mike's name as he went. Just as he reached the top, the current finally let go. My brother's body snapped free, bounced off the top rung, and Mike collapsed into my father's arms, knocking the breath out of them both and nearly sending them crashing to the ground. But somehow, my dad managed to hold on. He wrapped his arms around his son and gripped the ladder with all his might. They remained in that embrace for a long time, shaken and stunned, yet alive. Gradually, they started climbing back down until they reached the ground. At that moment, they just hugged and wept; it was a scary sight for everyone at the job site.

Electrical work wasn't just hard—it could kill you. And I knew then that I would never strap on a tool belt the way my father did during his 30+ years in the industry.

> *"It is not flesh and blood, but the heart, that makes us fathers and sons."*
> —Johann Friedrich von Schiller

The Pitfalls of High School

As my love for the ocean grew, my grades sank. Senior year was a blur. I can't remember much about being in class—but I remember the beach activities, bonfires, and senior pranks like they were yesterday. . .those are stories for another time. I took full advantage of the school's "work study" program, which meant I was off campus by 11:00 a.m. and heading straight to one of the jobs I held at the time.

Graduation loomed heavy, and that's when reality hit: I was failing a class I needed to graduate, World Studies, taught by Tony Sisca (*or Tony Babe, as he was often called*). The class was supposed to be easy, but somehow I managed to end the semester with an "F". How could that happen? I never saw Tony Babe take attendance, but he knew who was in class and who wasn't. My overall GPA was hanging right at 2.0, and if I didn't pass Mr. Sisca's class, I wouldn't graduate or walk with my peers. I was a dead man walking (or not walking). My parents were strict disciplinarians, and failure wasn't an option.

Grandparents, aunts, uncles, and cousins were all coming into town to celebrate, and I was going to embarrass my entire family. My dad had only made it through the tenth grade, so for both of us, finishing high school wasn't just a goal—it was a milestone.

With only two weeks left before school ended, I remember practically begging Mr. Sisca for a way to make things right. He thought for a moment, then said, "Write a paper summarizing the syllabus and the class. I'll decide after I read it." It was finals week, and I must've looked terrified, because he stopped me before I walked back to my seat and said, "Stay after class."

I waited until everyone had left the room and approached his desk,

"What happened, Dan?" he asked.

I was honest. I told him that I never saw him take attendance, and since everyone said he was kind and easy to pass, I thought I could slide by unnoticed.

We talked for about fifteen minutes, discussing class, my goals, and even a little about life outside of school. Then he started testing me with a few questions from the curriculum. To his surprise, I knew the answers. I told him I'd kept up with the reading because I still planned to pass the final. He smiled, realizing I hadn't quit; I'd just gambled on the wrong strategy.

"I know your family," he said. "And I understand what this moment means to them. I hope you have learned something from the choices that you made." Then he locked eyes with me. He was calm yet firm, full of compassion. Then he said:

"You're better than this. I am going to pass you. But you must promise me something: **Be More than This Moment.**"

Years later, I served as Chairman of the Dana Point Chamber of Commerce Education Committee, where I also held the position of Chamber President. By that time, I had earned my college degree and was working on my master's in business. I invited Tony to our annual scholarship luncheon and shared this story publicly with my peers and the students we were honoring that day.

It was a moment of personal redemption. It was emotional for every attendee, but especially Mr. Sisca. I had kept my promise, not just by graduating from college, but through creating better 'moments', and building a better life because of it. Mr. Sisca's simple act of belief in me, offered at a vulnerable time, changed my life forever and taught me a lesson about leadership. Tony taught me that we rarely see others for who they truly are; we see them through the lens of their current season. That's why it matters to pause, look past the moment, connect with the person, and then move forward, together.

Tony Sisca passed away in 2014, but his words have never left me. That quiet act of grace didn't just help me cross a stage; it set the course for a life shaped by second chances, relentless effort, and a deeper compassion for people.

My First Real Corporate Job

After high school, I enrolled at Saddleback Community College and met a gentleman who owned a small landscaping company in Lake Forest, CA. We hit it off and soon became partners, growing the business quickly. The money came in fast, but so did old habits. I started working more than I studied, and my grades quickly dropped; I found myself chasing something outside the structure of education. Money!

Eventually, I needed a reset. I switched to night classes so I could continue working, but I knew I had to get back on track academically. Slowly, I found balance. I righted the ship and graduated from Community College within three years. From there, I transferred to California State University, Fullerton, and around the same time, my girlfriend's father offered me a job at his civil engineering firm. I left the landscaping business and traded my muddy boots, tan, and chiseled physique for slacks, a sport coat, and a new kind of muscle—one built for meetings instead of manual labor.

I started working in the blueprint room at Hunsaker & Associates, which was literally the lowest rung on the corporate ladder. It was a job that made me proud. The sweet smell of ammonia hung in the air, but that position gave me access to everyone: civil engineers, planners, government relations managers, and the executive team. I stayed late whenever possible to pick up more hours and constantly asked questions, listened closely, and absorbed it all in. Within six months, I was training as a draftsman after my shift under the guidance of **Duane Cattanaugh, Gordon Farley, and Tom Gisler** (who referred to my work as *mylar carving*).

Soon, I began working full time for one of the partners, **Doug Snyder**, and eventually, I secured projects directly with **Richard Hunsaker**, the company's founder. Richard was a force of nature, standing 6'7" with a booming laugh and a giant heart. He was a man of deep Christian faith, unwavering integrity, and bold vision. Under his leadership, the company grew from 150 to over 500 employees, expanding across four satellite offices throughout California and into Las Vegas. Richard remained focused and driven as the business fluctuated in line with the economy and the number of projects in the pipeline. He earned the respect of everyone he met, and his status in the industry and reach within the business were legendary. He mentored everyone in the business, and he taught me that results and relationships aren't opposites; they're partners. Business is born in how people treat one another; it's about the laughter in the lunch room, and at the end of the day, closing up knowing that you have completed what you set out to do.

Culture at Hunsaker wasn't just encouraged, it was lived. The company held picnics every year at Doheny State Beach, where every employee (and their family members) left with a prize. Friday dance breaks to Todd Rundgren's *"Bang the Drum All Day,"* chili cook-offs, and costume parties for whatever crazy event was dreamed up were commonplace. Christmas parties came with generous bonuses and heartfelt recognitions. Individual wins were celebrated in front of the entire team, not just for performance, but for the heart behind the effort. It was ridiculous and unforgettable. Laughter and camaraderie filled the air, making work feel more like a party with family members than the daily grind of unrewarded work.

I had the great privilege of bonding with Mr. Hunsaker over books, John Grisham novels, short stories, University of

Southern California (USC) Football Trivia, leadership titles by John Maxwell, and countless others.

When someone left the company, it wasn't just a quiet exit. They got the complete treatment, playful callouts over the intercom, such as "John Smith, please call extension 419," or "John Smith, you're needed at the front desk," followed by "John Smith, your mom is here to pick you up." One after another, voices would chime in. The employees were smiling; everyone was in on the joke. It was silly, but it meant something. It was their way of saying, *you mattered here at H&A*. You weren't just clocking in and out, you were part of something. And for me, it was the first time I felt that working for a "professional" company didn't have to feel rigid or intimidating. It could be warm, special, even fun.

Dick Hunsaker passed away a few years ago. But like Tony Sisca, his impact still echoes in how I lead and serve. I am forever grateful for the way they mentored, cared for, and supported me as I grew into my various roles. Their lessons remain my foundation: lead with love, lift others, and build cultures that feel like home. Every time I am faced with a challenge or am confused to how I should react, I hear their voices reminding me why it matters.

The Promotion That Nearly Broke Me

As the economy began to wobble, I decided to leave my well-paying career as a Government Relations Manager and fully commit to finishing college. After ten grueling years of night classes and working full-time, I finally crossed the finish line. With a college degree in hand *(and a significantly better GPA than when I finished high school)*, I was ready to return to Hunsaker & Associates, seeking a better opportunity for growth; however, the timing was less than ideal. The industry was collapsing, and friends with big titles were suddenly out of work.

Still, I believed in momentum. I printed a hundred résumés and went door-to-door, shaking hands with whoever would take one. On an especially grueling day, I handed out about twenty-five résumés, and by nightfall, I had received a job offer from an environmental engineering firm.

Ironically, it wasn't my degree that got me hired—it was the formatting of my résumé. That attention to detail mattered more than I knew. My first assignment was translating dense technical reports into plain language for state and federal agencies. I was surrounded by scientists, engineers, and chemists working on environmental cleanup projects (*also known as CERCLA, which was tied to the Superfund legislation*). It was fascinating, high-stakes work, and a world away from where I started.

I was surrounded by some of the brightest minds in the country in this field of work, including engineers, chemists, and scientists, who studied the effects of past waste management practices.

The work included environmental cleanup projects, repairing damage to prevent groundwater contamination, installing PVC liners and leachate systems at older landfills nationwide, and identifying chemical plumes that had leaked from various factories and manufacturing facilities to determine who was responsible for the cleanup efforts. This was all part of the Superfund cleanup legislation, aimed at undoing decades of damage in the waste management industry and older manufacturing processes that had created contamination issues that were not fully understood at the time.

NOTE: *The Superfund cleanup legislation, also known as CERCLA (Comprehensive Environmental Response, Compensation, and Liability Act), was passed in 1980. Congress enacted it on December 11, 1980. The Superfund program was established to address the cleanup of hazardous waste sites and respond to environmental emergencies.*

As I was settling into the new role, I was on a rotation that had me working a Saturday morning. On my way to the copier, the Executive VP stopped me. "You need to avoid walking past the corner offices," he said. "It's distracting." It wasn't the comment itself that stuck; it was the undertone. A quiet assertion of hierarchy, a show of force to let me know who was in control, a reminder to stay in my lane. His words weren't about productivity; they were about power. And they carried the faint smell of ego masked as protocol.

As fate would have it, a few hours later, I noticed the CEO walk into his office just a few doors down from mine. His door was wide open, so I knocked and introduced myself, "Hello, I'm Daniel. I just wanted to thank you for the opportunity to be a part of your business." He smiled, stood up, and walked over to shake my hand. We chatted casually about work, family, sports, and life in general. He walked me through the history of how the business was started and what they were trying to achieve. That moment changed everything.

With lunchtime approaching, the office began to empty. I saw him in his office again and asked if he wanted anything to eat. "Just grab me a burger," he said, then paused. I replied, "Actually… how about Peppino's? I feel like eating some Italian food today."

"That would be great! Tell them you want the 'DE special.' They'll know," he replied.

I placed the food in his office while he was on a call. A few minutes later, he appeared at my desk. "Do you want to watch the USC football game?" We walked to his office and sat on a couch facing the television. A couple of hours into the game, the EVP walked in, froze, and left without a word. But that victory was short-lived, or so I thought.

That Monday morning, a message was waiting for me at the front desk: "Please report to HR." I braced for the worst.

"Dan, I understand you shared some time with the CEO this weekend. You need to pack up your office." I froze. Then came the twist:

"The CEO would like you to take the office outside his. You've been reassigned to work directly for him."

Working for him was exhilarating and brutal. He was in his seventies; I was in my twenties. We worked days that blurred into nights. I once logged thirty-seven straight hours, went home for a shower, and came back for eighteen more. He pushed me hard, but I learned to think fast, lead confidently, and hold my own under pressure.

Because of my new role, I was largely untouchable; even the Executive VP's infamous wrath couldn't touch me. He had a reputation for tearing people down, and I had watched grown professionals crumble under the pressure he placed on them. I wasn't immune to his tirades, but I never feared him. I knew my worth, and I had earned my seat at the table. But even armor cracks under enough pressure.

The EVP couldn't fire me, but he wanted to break me—and he tried. The constant tension wore me down. Over the next year, my health collapsed. Doctors began running tests. Bloodwork. Scans. They whispered "cancer," and for weeks, I lived with that fear while still showing up to work every day.

During one particular visit with a new doctor, he asked, "What do you do for a living?" After hearing my schedule, he paused and said, "I don't think this is cancer. It's stress. Let me run a few more tests."

When the results came in, my dad was there. He looked me in the eye and said simply, "You're done. It's time to move on." It wasn't advice, it was a lifeline.

When My World Went Quiet

Soon after, I left the firm and joined SOLAG Disposal, a family-owned waste management company based in South Orange County. It was founded in 1957 and run by Tom Trulis and his brother, Jim Koutroulis. The business understood the balance between profit and purpose. You would often see the owners chatting with residents, attending fundraisers, or meeting with city officials. For a young man trying to find his way after years of corporate intensity, it felt like home.

We started early each day, which suited me perfectly, as I've always been an early riser. The habit came from my dad, who rarely slept past 5:30 a.m. I would often hear him downstairs walking the floor, see the kitchen light glowing, and hear the click of the coffee pot. On occasion, I would join him for a quick conversation or just to hang out before the day began. On special mornings, we'd drive to Tommy's, a twenty-four-hour coffee shop in San Clemente, for breakfast before sunrise. I didn't realize how sacred the mornings would become, etched in my memory.

One particular morning began like any other. It was 4:30 a.m., and I was preparing for a community presentation at the Kiwanis Club. The prep was done, the notes were ready, and for once, I had time to spare. It felt like the perfect morning to see my dad before the day got going. He always appreciated a quick visit, and I had plenty of time.

Then the phone rang.

It was just after 5:30 a.m. when I answered, and all I heard was my mother's voice. It came through the line fractured and unrecognizable, wrapped in pain I couldn't comprehend. Between sobs, she managed to say, "Just come."

"Your dad…"

My blood ran cold.

I dropped everything and bolted out the door, heart pounding, driving like the world was on fire. When I arrived, the front door was open. My mom was running from room to room with her hands on her head, lost in panic.

Her voice cracked like glass, "The garage," she said through the tears.

I walked into the garage, not understanding the direction. That's where I found my father. He had taken his own life.

Time stopped. I moved on instinct as shock consumed me. It was mechanical, detached, and desperate, followed by a level of fear so deep it felt as if I would drown in the grief. I picked up my father, called 911, and performed CPR through tears and disbelief.

There was no pulse. No breath. No second chance. After a stretch of chest compressions that felt both endless and too short, I stopped. The dispatcher kept talking, but there was nothing left to say while I tried to make sense of a scene that would never make sense.

"Just send the coroner," I told her.

The rest of the day unfolded like a scene from someone else's life–police, medics, flashing lights. What most people don't realize is that every suicide triggers an investigation. It doesn't matter how clear things seem; the process is clinical, procedural, and unbearable for those left behind. Almost immediately, the officers separated my mother and me, asking for timelines and details while I stood there, numb, watching neighbors gather outside. It felt like being trapped in a nightmare I couldn't wake from.

At one point, my mom broke down completely. Without thinking, I got up from my chair and stood between her and the police officers, and said quietly, but firmly, "You need to leave. Now!" It was a tense moment that could have escalated quickly, but to their credit, they understood. The officers that day were kind, patient, and compassionate. They have a brutal job, and in hindsight, I can see the weight they carried walking into a moment like that. We weren't strangers as we'd been part of this small community for more than forty years. Some had known our family for decades, which only deepened the ache in the room.

In the days that followed, my good friend, Wyatt Hart, the Chief of Police in a nearby town, called me personally when he heard the news. He quickly became our anchor, helping to guide our family through every painful step. Wyatt checked in often, making sure my mother and I were holding up. We can never repay the kindness and compassion that he extended to our family. Wyatt was the foundation when the ground beneath us had completely given way. His presence reminded me that even in tragedy, love still finds a way.

The weeks that followed were a blur. I barely spoke, as if the breath of life had been pulled straight out of me. I moved through each day in a fog. Time lost all meaning. Work disappeared from my mind. I stopped answering calls. I just...existed. Friends came and went, but I barely remember who stopped by. Yet one visitor stands out vividly in my memory.

Understanding the Importance of Friendships

A few days after my dad's passing, my boss, Jim Koutroulis, the President of SOLAG Disposal, showed up at our door with his son Tommy. They didn't just stop by; they *showed up*. Jim hugged me, looked me in the eyes, and said, "You don't look so good, Dan. How are you holding up? The entire company heard about what happened, and we are worried about you.

Clean yourself up and get back to work on Monday. We'll figure it out together. You just need to keep busy."

I didn't know how to respond, but I was back at work the following Monday. Jim came into my office, sat down, and said,
"I don't care if you do anything, just be here. When you are
ready, start working. My door's always open."

So there I sat, silent, just staring out the window as the trucks
moved in and out of the yard. I didn't type. I didn't talk. I just
existed. As the days moved on, something began to shift.
Conversations started slowly but began to capture momentum.
Soon, I realized that I was surrounded by people who cared,
and that was the catalyst to feeling normal again.

The entire company stood alongside me. My co-workers
checked in, drove me home when I wasn't okay, and sat beside
me in silence when words weren't enough. Even when I made
poor decisions born from grief, they didn't walk away. They
stayed. Their quiet loyalty and love brought me back to life.

So many people played a pivotal role in helping me to over-
come the mental battle I faced; however, one of the major
turning points occurred a couple of years later. Two people
helped me find my footing again: Penny Maynard and Kirk
Lapple.

Just a week before my father passed, I had been elected
President of the Dana Point Chamber of Commerce. Over
the next few years, Penny and Kirk helped me navigate the
Chamber business, ensuring I was prepared, supported, and
looked confident and polished. On the outside, I tried to perform the part: smiling, showing up to Grand Openings, giving
presentations, and keeping the machine moving. But Penny
and Kirk saw through it; inside, I was fractured.

One afternoon, they invited me to lunch and some small talk.
Penny leaned in gently. "Dan. . .it looks like smiling hurts."

"It does, Penny," I said. "I don't know how to come back from this."

That opened the door for Kirk, "We're worried about you. We miss the old Dan, the one whose joy and laughter could brighten any room. Don't let it slip away. Find your smile again."

There was something healing in their care. I left that lunch changed. Their words didn't erase the pain, but they reminded me I was still surrounded by love. That truth didn't fix everything, but it helped me take one step forward. I owed it to them—and to myself—to try to find my way back.

When Adam Sandler was being awarded the Mark Twain Prize, David Spade got up to speak about his friend. At one point, David shared that when Kate took her life, many people were scared to call him because they didn't know what to say. Adam Sandler, however, went to Spade's house.

David didn't answer his door for Adam, but Adam wouldn't leave, so he finally opened it. Adam "whispered" to him, "Hey, yo, yo. Oh, depression". Spade said this was "what [he] needed to hear at the time" and that it broke the tension.

Acquaintances send a text. Friends show up.

My dad was kind, funny, and endlessly curious. He was my mentor, my sidekick, and my best friend, and they all rolled into one. We watched movies, played ping-pong, and talked about everything from faith to music to life. His death still doesn't make sense. But I've learned to hold on to the *fullness* of his life rather than the pain of that moment.

He wasn't just a contractor; he was a Korean War veteran, a man who'd worn both a hard hat and a uniform. Both professions, tragically, carry some of the highest suicide rates in America. Veterans are taught to carry the weight. Construction workers are told to tough it out. That silence can be deadly. Somewhere in it, my dad got lost.

We don't talk enough about mental health in those worlds; the invisible wounds soldiers bring home, or the strain of grinding through pressure without an outlet. My dad would've done anything for his family, his crew, or his country. He just didn't know how to ask for help when it was his turn to be carried.

The coroner's report revealed painful gallstones. Maybe he feared something worse. Perhaps the pain, physical, emotional, spiritual, just became too much. I'll never fully know. But I know this: his life mattered.

And so does the conversation we still need to have.

I miss his advice, his laugh, his presence. His death broke me, but it also broke me *open*. It re-centered my life around what truly matters: people, purpose, and love.

Work isn't separate from life; it's part of it. Too often, we blur the lines in the wrong direction, prioritizing career over the callings that make us human—sons, daughters, parents, and friends. Work matters; it gives meaning, stability, and a place to build, but it isn't everything.

For leaders, responsibility goes beyond profit or process. It's about creating environments where people grow into who they're meant to be. Train them well, not just in skill, but in heart. Encourage them and invest in them. In the end, the legacy of work isn't what we build; it's who we build *up* along the way.

Reflection and Change in an Uncertain Moment in Time

Before my father's death, our family was a force: tight-knit, loyal, and bound by love. We shared everything: dreams, struggles, and laughter that filled every room. His loss shattered that unity in ways we couldn't have imagined. The heart that held us together was gone, and what remained looked the same from the outside, but the pulse had changed. The fabric of our family unraveled, and the closeness we once took for granted slipped out of reach. That's true in leadership, too: appearance can deceive. You have to look deeper, listen harder, and notice what's missing beneath the surface.

My story began with dirt under my fingernails, shaped by long days, hard work, and a father who believed his three sons would one day take over his business, just as he'd watched the Rohans build theirs. That was his dream. But life had other plans. I didn't inherit his company, but I inherited his spirit to go and build my own legacy.

A year after his passing, I left SOLAG Disposal to chart my own course. The Koutroulis family had shown me what real leadership looked like—loyalty, grit, and an unshakable commitment to people. They redefined for me what culture truly means. For a while, I thought I might retire there, surrounded by the team that helped carry me through the darkest chapter of my life. But when the company was sold, I knew it was time to move on.

Grief reshapes your vision. It strips away the noise and leaves you searching for something deeper. I no longer cared about the next title or paycheck; I cared about purpose. About building something that outlives you.

Over time, I learned that when people or organizations lead with purpose, the bottom line strengthens. Purpose doesn't just motivate; it unites. And alignment built on love drives results that money never will.

My father's death left a scar, but it also gave me clarity. It reminded me that even in the darkest moments, love still wins. Every sunrise is a chance to lead with gratitude, and to live the kind of life God intended: one driven by purpose, not ego.

> *"You never know how strong you are until being strong is the only choice you have."*
>
> —Bob Marley

CHAPTER 3

Foundations Forged in Family, Culture, and Loss

"We inherit more than names from those we love—we inherit the unfinished stories they leave behind."

Walking the Camino: Making Memories with My Mother

When my mother turned 83, we embarked on a dream together: walking the Camino de Santiago, also known as "The Way." This ancient pilgrimage stretches across Spain, culminating at the Cathedral of Santiago de Compostela, where tradition holds that the remains of Saint James the Apostle are buried.

Our inspiration came from Richard Hunsaker, who had walked the Camino several times. He described it as a transformative experience, saying, "Dan, once you take the walk, you will fight to get back every year to experience something different." His words resonated deeply, and we finally decided to undertake the trek ourselves.

Preparing for the Camino was daunting. The full route, known as the Camino Francés, begins in Saint-Jean-Pied-de-Port, France, and spans approximately 770 kilometers (about 480 miles) to Santiago de Compostela. Given our circumstances, we opted for a shorter segment, starting from Sarria, which still qualified us for the Compostela certificate awarded to pilgrims who complete at least the last one hundred kilometers on foot.

I'll admit, I was underprepared, but there was no turning back. My eighty-three-year-old mother was ready, and we were in it together.

The first few days were beautiful but brutal. The sun was hot, the hills endless, and by the second day, my knees had swollen, and my feet were covered in blisters. Yet, every "Buen Camino" from fellow travelers reminded me why we were there. The Camino isn't just a path; it's a pilgrimage of the soul.

Each day presented new challenges and rewards. We traversed rolling hills, walked through ancient villages, and crossed streams, sharing meals with people from around the *world. The Camino is more than a physical path; it's a tapestry of stories, cultures, and personal revelations.*

One of the most sacred moments came at the Cruz de Ferro, a tall iron cross atop a mound of stones left by pilgrims before us. Each person carries a rock they picked up at the beginning of their journey, representing either a burden or a prayer. The area was filled with pilgrims in prayer, crying, or seated, emotionally and physically exhausted from the path they had encountered. Our stone carried the weight of my father's loss, our faith, doubts, and the desire to live a life filled with love. When we placed it down, we didn't just leave a stone; we left the part of ourselves that needed to carry it.

By the time we reached Santiago de Compostela, our bodies were broken, but our hearts were full. My mother wept as we stood before the cathedral; so did I. What began as a physical challenge became a journey of healing, faith, and love.

Now at 91, my mom still talks about the Camino, the food, the laughter, the strangers who became friends, and the locals who offered fruit, water, and encouragement along the way. For me, it was proof that resilience grows stronger when shared.

On the trail, progress isn't about speed; it's about pace, company, and what you choose to carry. People go farther when someone believes in them. Rituals matter ("Buen Camino" became fuel), and clear markers can prevent drift. And when the load is heavy, you don't muscle through it alone; you share the weight. Leadership, it turns out, is a pilgrimage: set the pace, see the people, and keep the culture moving in the right direction.

Someday, I plan to return and walk the longer Via de la Plata from Seville, a journey of more than 1,000 kilometers that offers reflection and renewal. But no journey, no matter how long, will ever compare to the one I shared with my mother.

Culture Emboldened

The Camino didn't just renew my spirit; it reframed my perspective on leadership. Every step was a reminder that progress, whether on a trail or in a company, is built one relationship, one act of belief, or one shared purpose at a time. The lessons I carried from that path would soon follow me into the business world, where culture, too, becomes a journey of faith, endurance, and connection.

In business, the "markers" are values, the "companions" are our teams, and the "pace" is the operating rhythm leaders set every day. The first place the lesson was tested was within a large, disciplined system. McDonald's is where I saw how standards, people, and pace create culture.

McDonald's, for all its burgers and fries, had something I hadn't fully experienced yet: a large corporate culture at a publicly traded business. McDonald's was serious about execution, about brand standards, and creating an experience for both customers and employees. It wasn't just about serving food; it was about serving consistency, community, and pride in their brand.

It was there that I met Don Ikeler, who would become a very influential mentor throughout my career. Although ten years my junior, Don had a rare gift of balancing high expectations with genuine care. Leadership, to him, was never about power or title; it was about service.

He had a wicked sense of humor, even amid chaos, and taught me that vulnerability is permission to breathe. I watched him navigate construction setbacks, cost overruns, and city requirements that shifted overnight. No matter the crisis, Don remained calm and focused on solutions, not blame.

His role extended beyond handling field issues. Don also managed up to McDonald's leadership, whose priorities centered on accountability and execution. I quickly learned that delays on the ground rippled through the entire business, impacting our department, the brand's profitability, and beyond. Each hiccup wasn't isolated; it affected the broader organization in ways I hadn't fully appreciated before.

Several years into my role as an Area Construction Manager for McDonald's, Don transitioned to CKE Restaurants, the parent company of Carl's Jr. and Hardee's. Within months of his joining the brand, he reached out one day and asked if I would like to run Franchise Development for Carl's Jr. I met Don, along with Dave McDivett, and we sat down to discuss life, family, and our paths into the industry. Not once did they mention the role. At the end of lunch, they slid a job description across the table, and I barely glanced at it. I simply told them, "I'll start in three weeks."

Over the next ten years, I had the opportunity to work under the leadership of Rich Buxton *(Executive VP, whom I had known from McDonald's)*, Jack Willingham *(VP of Development)*, and the two Daves *(Dave McDivett and David Luxton)*. During this period, I learned invaluable lessons in the QSR business, from development and construction to managing challenges with the right mindset. Just six months after I started at CKE Restaurants, Don left the company and joined Chick-fil-A, where he remains employed today. We continue to talk regularly.

The team at CKE Restaurants taught me to see each shop from a customer's perspective. I learned how my role affects annual sales, the ability for teams to hire for opening day, stock products, and ensure a smooth handoff with the facilities team. I remember one time when I was panicking over a paint scheme and had some other concerns about one of my builds. In this industry, 'branding' and presenting a strong product are essential, so I didn't want to turn over a project I wasn't proud of. The delay was causing internal issues with the Operations Team, which was also trying to meet its goals.

Dave Luxton and I went out and walked the site together with my construction punch list in hand. When we reached the area where I was struggling to 'let go,' Dave paused and said, "Yeah, this doesn't look right. But let me ask you a question, Dan, do you think a customer will notice?" "Probably not," I replied. "Do you think we will sell any fewer burgers unless this gets corrected?" Again, I said, "Probably not." I soon realized that the goal was not to accept mediocrity but to focus on the right battles.

That day, I learned the art of discernment, the balance between perfection and progress. The goal isn't to lower standards; it's to fight for what truly matters.

By my ninth year at CKE, I took a detour into sign sales—a lucrative but hollow move. The money was good, but something essential was missing. Purpose had been replaced by profit. That misstep, however, led to one of the most meaningful friendships of my career.

This slight detour introduced me to Aaron Harris, an executive at Popeyes Fried Chicken. We connected regularly over construction, development, and yes, purchasing signs. After sharing meals and conversations, his dedication to excellence became clear. Aaron often said, "One day we're going to work together and set a brand on fire." I didn't know what he meant at the time, but I never forgot it. He was tough, direct, and unfiltered. You always knew where you stood, which, in leadership, is a rare and invaluable quality.

People who know Aaron understand he is a force. A rare mix of sharp intelligence and relentless work ethic, he stands 6'7", and he literally towers over a room. His laughter could light it up, but his no-nonsense drive to succeed makes him, and the brands he has touched, remarkably successful. At first, it was intimidating to be in his presence. But as I got to know him, I saw beyond the toughness. That same intensity, which could feel overwhelming, was also what made him one of the best friends you could ever hope for. He never missed a call. He was tough on people, yes, but if you needed someone in your corner to navigate a deal, land a job, or get out of a tight spot, Aaron is that guy. You just have to be ready for a blunt response that is sometimes brutal, but always honest. I came to admire and respect that honesty, even when it was hard to hear.

Thanks to that very relationship, more than ten years after we met, the most significant opportunity of my career arrived.

Dutch Bros: Finding the Unicorn

Aaron had begun consulting for Dutch Bros Coffee, helping prepare the company for rapid growth. "You need to meet these guys," he said.

Sitting down with Travis Boersma and his brother-in-law, Brian Maxwell, was more than just a professional meeting; it was a glimpse into something sacred. They didn't speak of Dutch Bros as a business, but as a legacy that was alive and expanding. To them, it wasn't just a brand; it was a tribute to Travis's late brother, Dane "The Wise Man" Boersma, the elder brother, the dreamer, and the culture-setter. He was the heartbeat that breathed life into their company.

In 2005, Dane was diagnosed with ALS (*also known as Lou Gehrig's disease*), a devastating neurodegenerative illness. Despite the challenges, his spirit never faltered, and his influence continued to inspire everyone around him. When he passed in 2009 at just fifty-five years old, the loss reverberated through his family, the employees, and the community. Every aspect of Dutch Bros, from how they lead to how they serve, is rooted in Dane's philosophy: putting people first, building community, and always leading with love.

That spirit was felt immediately. What I thought would be a traditional interview turned into an influential human conversation that was unlike any I ever had in the business world. We spoke about purpose, about building something that matters, and then the conversation shifted, quietly and unexpectedly, from business to something far more personal.

We began talking about Dane's battle with ALS, and how it shaped not only the business but also Travis and Brian personally. I shared my own experience of losing my father to suicide, and although two very different stories, both were defined by love, loss, and the haunting ache of moments left unfinished. The energy in the room shifted, not because it was expected, but because grief has a way of stepping in uninvited, leaving its mark when you least expect it.

For a few powerful moments, we weren't an executive, a founder, or a candidate. We were a brother and a son, two men honoring the lives that shaped us, and ultimately made us who we are. At one point, our eyes welled up with tears. Two grown men caught in a moment of raw vulnerability, grieving and remembering what 'could have been'. We understood that some moments in life slip by and can never be reclaimed, and we both knew the weight that carried with it.

Shortly after the interview, I was offered a role at Dutch Bros, and what I discovered inside the company was even more beautiful than I had imagined. Working at the company wasn't just a job; it was a transformational experience. It solidified my belief in what's possible when culture is done right. Culture is the catalyst for success. During my time at Dutch Bros, I would often tell people that "I had found the unicorn." Because that's what it was, finding a place where business and love, profit and purpose, ambition and authenticity, all lived together under one roof.

The Heartbeat of Dutch Bros

The story of Dutch Bros started like so many great American dreams—with humble beginnings, family grit, and a whole lot of hustle. The company was founded by two brothers, Dane and Travis Boersma, who were third-generation dairy farmers living in Grants Pass, Oregon. In 1990, the government passed new regulations that required their family to change their farming practices, making it impossible for them to stay in business. The family made the difficult decision to shut down the farm and explore new avenues for survival.

At the same time, coffee was becoming more than just a morning ritual; it had become an experience. The market was shifting from simple drip brews to handcrafted drinks layered with flavor and personality. But it wasn't just about what was in the cup; it was about who was behind the counter. People weren't just buying coffee; they were building relationships. Coffee shops were becoming community hubs where customers came to connect, recharge, and start their day with a smile.

And just like that, the spark was lit. It was 1992, and Dutch Bros was born–though the word *born* might be too fancy. They didn't have a shiny shopfront or a grand opening. They had a pop-up tent, a pushcart, and a handshake with a local shopping center owner who allowed them to set up outside. They weren't baristas. . .They were Bro-istas (Broistas), a name that has stuck and grown with the brand.

The first day's take? $67.25.

But in those few crumpled bills and coins, they saw something more: the seeds of a dream.

Dirty hands and back-breaking work were replaced by rock 'n' roll music, great coffee, and a vibrant connection with the community. Travis often tells stories about the road to those first milestones; stories of burnt coffee beans, terrible drink ideas, selling franchises to friends and family, and even surviving a devastating fire at their newly built roasting facility. The common thread? Resilience, heart, and the fierce belief that if they leaned into love, they couldn't lose.

After the tragic loss of Dane, Travis didn't retreat; he doubled down. He would often ask himself, "How do I honor my brother?" How do I build something even bigger, even better, in his memory?

The answer was culture, combined with a relentless dedication to serving others.

Today, Dane's legacy is still very much alive in the halls, hearts, and habits of Dutch Bros. Each year, the brand celebrates "Drink One for Dane," raising millions of dollars for ALS research and patient care. As of this writing, over $10.3 million has been raised—not just money, but memory, honor, and hope.

Dane's presence still fills every Dutch Bros shop, every "Have a killer day!" shouted across a drive-thru window, and every act of kindness that starts with a smile. Each year, the company celebrates *Drink One for Dane*, raising millions for ALS research and patient care. As of this writing, more than $10 million has been raised.

After Dane's passing, the company made a pivotal choice: to stop selling franchises and transition to an operator-led model. Similar to In-N-Out Burger and Chick-fil-A, the goal wasn't control, but cultural preservation. Leadership understood that protecting the brand's heart meant ensuring its values were lived, not licensed.

Instead of expansion through ownership, Dutch Bros chose expansion through *leadership*. The company began developing people from within, creating what they call "compelling futures" for their employees. Those who exemplify the brand are trained to become operators and are offered a generous salary, profit-sharing, territory ownership, and leadership roles, all rooted in the same promise to *make a massive difference, one cup at a time.*

The shift to an operator model didn't just change the business; it redefined how the company connected with its customers. What started as a commitment to the culture became an everyday rhythm that kept the heart of the brand alive through its people.

Continuing the Vibe

Before COVID-19 reshaped the world, lunch was brought in for everyone. Executives ate side by side with employees–no one sat alone, and no title mattered. It wasn't just a meal; it was a daily reminder that connection fuels culture. Meetings followed a consistent rhythm: open, collaborative, and honest. Ideas flowed, disagreements were welcome, and people left feeling heard.

Though the cadence of shared meals has changed, Dutch Bros never lost sight of what truly propels the brand forward–connection.

Then came Friday's **"Dub Shots."** Each week, employees would gather with small cups of espresso to celebrate wins, milestones, and the moments that defined the week. They'd read stories from customers, honor Broistas who made an impact, and lift their glasses to a job well done. By the end, there were usually a few tears–because those stories weren't about sales or performance; they were about people. The unseen acts of kindness that built the company's

And then. . .there was **COACHA!**

I was fortunate to attend the last two COACHA events Dutch Bros hosted, and they remain the most powerful company gatherings I've ever witnessed. Imagine a full-day celebration that fuses purpose with pure joy–featuring motivational speakers like Simon Sinek and Alex Banayan, breakout sessions, food trucks, giveaways, music, and laughter filling every corner.

Everywhere you look, people share their talents: art, music, a skill, and a smile. Leadership recognized Broistas who made an impact that year. Teams competed and cheered each other on, and when night fell, it all culminated in a concert featuring major artists like Macklemore, AJR, and others.

It felt like part rock show, part TED Talk, part revival. By the end of the event, people were sent back to their shops fired up. Reminding them that work doesn't have to drain your soul, but it can positively impact lives at all levels of the organization.

These events weren't cheap, but their impact was immeasurable. They reminded everyone what Dutch Bros stands for: people first, always. Even as the company grew to 25,000 employees, the spirit never dimmed. COVID-19 may have paused live gatherings, but it didn't break the rhythm. The heartbeat of Dutch Bros still pulses strong.

The real secret of Dutch Bros' success isn't coffee—it's their unwavering commitment to serving others. It's the same spirit that began with two brothers, Dane and Travis Boersma, who chose connection over convention. Their authenticity, love for people, and respect for community are brewed into every cup.

Dutch Bros gets it right every day by living a simple truth:

If you love your people well, they'll love your brand fiercely.

The Inverse Pyramid in Action

Dutch Bros built its culture on a leadership philosophy that inverted the traditional hierarchy. Inspired in part by an article from the 2008 Harvard Business Review, Dutch Bros employs an "inverted pyramid" leadership model. Shop employees *(the Broistas)* and store teams are at the top, backed by layers of management, leadership, and the CEO below. Leadership is about lifting people from below rather than directing from above.

The **traditional pyramid structure in business** is a **hierarchical model** used to organize communication and responsibility within an organization. Authority and information flow from the CEO down through layers of management. It reflects how power and decision-making are concentrated at the top and gradually trickle down through the ranks. Often, ideas get lost in translation or diluted.

Figure 1. The Traditional Corporate Pyramid

While the traditional pyramid offers clarity and control, it can also create bottlenecks in decision-making and can lead to a disconnect between leadership and front-line workers. This feeling of separation or hierarchical gap can also affect morale and engagement among employees.

Vineet Nayar, in his book *Employees First, Customers Second*, popularized this inversion through his transformation of HCL Technologies. His model positioned employees at the top and management beneath them, holding them accountable for their success.[2] He introduced ideas such as reverse accountability (leaders are evaluated by how well they serve their teams), radical transparency (open sharing of performance data), and a focus on the value zone, which is the intersection where employees directly impact the customer. The result was faster learning, deeper engagement, and stronger outcomes. These elements are documented in HBS/Harvard Business Publishing materials and academic cases on HCL's transformation.[3]

The inverted pyramid structure is a people-first leadership model that inverts the traditional hierarchy.

[2] Nayar, V. Employees first, customers second: Turning conventional management upside down. Harvard Business Review Press. Harvard Business Review Store, 2010; Nayar, V. Put Your Employees First. Harvard Business Review, July 20, 2010. https://hbr.org/2010/07/put-your-employees-first; HCL Technologies. Key Concepts from Employees First, Customers Second. HCL Tech, 2022. https://www.hcltech.com/sites/default/files/documents/resources/brochure/files/emplyeesfirstminibook.pdf
[3] Hill, L. A., Khanna, T., & Stecker, E. A., HCL Technologies. Harvard Business School Case No. 9-408-004. Harvard Business School Publishing. The Case Centre, HEC Paris, 2008.

Figure 2. The Inverted Corporate Pyramid

Nayar institutionalized "reverse accountability" *(where managers are evaluated based on how effectively they serve employees)*, radical transparency *(sharing financial and performance data openly)*, and internal service levels. Decision rights and problem-solving shift toward the "value zone," which is where employees interact with customers; senior leaders focus on removing obstacles and enabling speed. These elements are documented in HBS/Harvard Business Publishing materials and academic cases on HCL's transformation.[4]

Dutch Bros demonstrates a practical version of this approach. This model is most evident with the Broistas. While their mission emphasizes the customer, their operating system essentially places Broistas at the top of the hierarchy to create daily customer experiences. They are the heartbeat of the brand, engaging directly with guests, understanding their needs, and spreading joy every day. They are the most essential part of the organization. Empowered to make real-time decisions, whether it's rewarding a drink, spending a little more time with a customer who needs encouragement, or embodying the brand's values through warmth, humility, and support.

Supervisors, middle managers, senior leadership, and the executive team exist to facilitate the customer-Broista experience, eliminate obstacles, and protect throughput and culture. Middle managers act more as mentors, coaches, and problem solvers to help their teams succeed. Executives focus on serving the organization (servant leaders), listening, providing resources, ensuring alignment with values, and cultivating the culture from the ground up. The CEO serves at the foundation of the organization, nurturing people, wisely allocating resources, and safeguarding the mission and identity of the brand, while ensuring the company's values are consistently reflected at all levels. They then clearly communicate that vision to stakeholders, shareholders, the media, and the broader industry. In other words, leadership supports the front line so the front line can serve the guest.

In this model, Broistas aren't just employees; when executed well, this ripple effect creates employees who feel empowered

---

[4] Hill, L. A., Khanna, T., & Stecker, E. A., HCL Technologies. Harvard Business School Case No. 9-408-004. Harvard Business School Publishing. The Case Centre, HEC Paris, 2008.

and take responsibility, customers who feel valued, and a culture that becomes a strategic advantage, one that competitors can't replicate.

Building a brand that lasts, not just one that performs, but one that resonates with your employees and customers, is what culture is all about. At Dutch Bros, I saw firsthand what happens when you lead with love. When you believe in your team, they trust your mission; when you serve your people, they serve your customers.

My time at Dutch Bros didn't just reshape my thinking around leadership; it reconnected me to why I chose business in the first place. Not just to build things, rack up profits, and scale the ladder, but the opportunity to connect with people, understand them, and lift them to their fullest potential.

As we move forward in this book, we'll explore exactly how to build this kind of culture—one rooted in clarity, kindness, and conviction. One where expectations are high, but humanity is never lost. Because love and strength aren't opposites. They're partners. You already have what it takes to lead differently. The only question is: are you brave enough to flip the pyramid?

Business, at its best, isn't just about what we make; it's about who we become while making it.

> *"What you leave behind is not what is engraved in stone monuments, but what is woven into the lives of others."*
> —Pericles

CHAPTER 4

Culture Isn't About Credit; It's About Contribution

"People don't care how much you know until they know how much you care."

—Theodore Roosevelt

Love in Action: The $4,600 Lesson

Few things were more powerful than an unforgettable moment during my time with Dutch Bros, which occurred at our annual COACHA event—a high-energy, daylong celebration of our people, our progress, and our purpose. COACHA was a movement, a chance to pour into our Broistas—the lifeblood of our brand—and remind them how much they mattered.

That day, halfway through the event, the room was alive with excitement as our co-founder, Travis Boersma, opened the floor for questions. A young Broista stepped up to the microphone. She looked nervous, her hands trembling slightly, but her voice remained steady.

"I'm struggling," she began. "I love my job here—I love this company, the people I work with, and the opportunities ahead. But I also want to continue my college education, and to do that, I would have to leave Dutch Bros and move back home. I don't know what to do."

The room went quiet. You could feel the impact of her honesty as everyone leaned in to see how Travis would answer.

Travis took a breath and responded with heart. "We value you. We're delighted to have you on the team. And yes, your education is important. If going back to school is your path, we offer our full support. And when you graduate, you'll always have a place at Dutch Bros."

The young woman's eyes welled up with tears.

"I just don't want to leave," she said. "But I need money to finish school."

And then, something incredible happened.

From the back of the room, someone shouted: **"What's your Venmo?"**

The entire room lit up.

Travis invited her on stage, and moments later, her Venmo QR code was projected on the big screen behind them. Another voice called out:
"How much do you need to finish school?"
She responded, "About $4,600."

That's all it took.

Within minutes, her fellow Broistas (her peers) poured their love into action. Donation after donation came in. There was no hesitation; just people helping one another. Within moments, she had the full amount, and then some.

It was never just about the money; it was about belonging to something bigger. What began as Dane's philosophy more than thirty years ago still resonates through the brand today, not because it has been preserved in name only, but because leaders and team members alike have embraced it, lived it, and passed it on. The simple idea of loving others remains the foundation—and that's what makes the culture feel alive.

That young woman left with more than just tuition; she left knowing she was valued and loved. That's what Dutch Bros is all about. It is not merely a brand but a culture that leads with compassion and follows through with action. That moment was instinctive, an impulse to serve others that wasn't learned from a training manual. It happened because love is an inherent part of the brand, demonstrated from the ground up.

That moment will stay with me forever. It was everything good about humanity wrapped up in one act of generosity. And it all started because of one young woman's courage to speak up.

That day was a revelation. It showed that when love becomes part of the operating system, it multiplies. It becomes contagious. That's the kind of leadership we're here to talk about, the kind that measures success by how people show up for each other when it counts most.

What happened that day captured the essence of this chapter: love as a leadership advantage. Because love, when lived with intention, doesn't make teams softer—it makes them stronger.

Love Is Not Weak; It's Powerful

A common mistake people make when hearing about "leading with love" is assuming it's a soft, feel-good philosophy that lowers standards or avoids accountability. But love in leadership isn't weak. It's fierce. It's disciplined. And it's deeply committed to helping people rise.

Love, when applied to leadership, isn't passive; it's a powerful tool in your cultural arsenal. It's bold, unwavering, and demands the best from people because it believes in them. Leading with love means challenging individuals to grow because you see their potential long before they do.

This kind of leadership doesn't lower expectations or avoid hard conversations. Instead, it pairs high standards with deep support. It gives employees the confidence to take risks, learn from their mistakes, and grow without fear of failure. Their responsibility? To show up with consistency, humility, and a commitment to becoming their best selves.

The greatest leaders prove that love isn't the opposite of performance; it's the strategy that drives it. From airlines to factories, entertainment to coffee shops, those who lead with love didn't weaken their organizations. They made them unstoppable.

Herb Kelleher: The Architect of Love-Based Leadership

Herb Kelleher, the legendary founder of Southwest Airlines, wasn't just running an airline; he was building a people-first movement before it was trendy.

He famously said, *"If you treat your people right, they'll treat your customers right."*

Simple? Sure. But revolutionary in an industry obsessed with metrics, control, and cost-cutting. Herb wasn't dismissing standards. Southwest was (*and still is*) impressively operational. But he led with humor, humanity, and heart. He cracked jokes, flew coach with the passengers, treated baggage handlers with the same respect he gave to executives, and loved his people. In return, his team loved him back with loyalty and performance that no bonus structures alone could have fostered.

The result? A wildly successful airline with unmatched employee retention, customer satisfaction, and profitability in one of the harshest industries around.

Leading with love didn't soften Southwest Airlines. It made the company invincible.

But this principle isn't confined to hospitality or customer-facing industries. Even in the hard edges of manufacturing, love has the power to transform both people and profits. Bob Chapman is proof of that.

Bob Chapman: Business as a Family Legacy

Another insightful masterclass comes from Bob Chapman of Barry-Wehmiller, a global manufacturing giant. In his book *Everybody Matters*, Chapman discusses how he transformed a struggling industrial company into a thriving enterprise simply by treating every team member like family. He didn't see employees as mere units of production but as human beings entrusted to his care. That meant investing in their growth, listening to their voices, and celebrating their lives beyond the factory floor.

As a result, productivity increased, turnover decreased, and profitability rose. Chapman demonstrated that you don't have to choose between caring about people and caring about performance. They are the same.

Chapman demonstrated that caring for people and prioritizing performance are not opposites, but rather two sides of the same coin. And if love means valuing people deeply, it also means being willing to have the tough conversations. That's where Walt Disney's approach comes in.

Walt Disney: Embracing Conflict

As we discussed earlier, love doesn't avoid difficult conversations; it embraces them. True love in leadership involves caring enough to address issues, listening when things aren't working, and creating space for uncomfortable truths. Love, at its highest level, welcomes feedback—not to defend ourselves, but to grow because of it. That's why some of the greatest leaders don't just tolerate conflict; they welcome it as a tool for progress. Walt Disney was one such leader.

Walt saw conflict and complaints as opportunities for improvement. He embraced a concept called "plussing," which involved continuously enhancing ideas and experiences. Instead of dismissing complaints from employees or guests, Disney considered them valuable signals and opportunities to improve the organization and demonstrate that people were heard. This method fostered a culture where feedback was not only appreciated but actively encouraged, leading to ongoing modernization and refinement of the Disney experience.

This philosophy aligns with Disney's broader commitment to excellence. By fostering a culture of "supportive conflict," Disney believed that the best ideas come from an environment where team members feel safe to express differing opinions and challenge the status quo. This approach was key in driving the creative processes that led to many of Disney's groundbreaking achievements.

Disney's method of plussing showed that love doesn't shield us from conflict; instead, it uses conflict to build something better. And that insight leads to a larger truth: culture itself doesn't survive by accident. If love is the foundation, then culture is the house it builds. Without daily care, it crumbles. With it, businesses can thrive even in the midst of a crisis.

Culture Doesn't Survive by Accident

The most challenging lesson to learn as a leader is that culture doesn't survive on good intentions alone. It must be actively nurtured to thrive. Culture is the invisible current flowing through every meeting, hallway conversation, and decision, big or small. Without intentional leadership, culture gradually erodes under the pressures of growth, stress, and change. Even the strongest culture will begin to weaken at the edges if it's not actively cared for and protected daily.

At Dutch Bros, it was never an afterthought; it was tangible. You could feel it the moment you walked through the door. It pulsed through the music in the front office and the laughter in the common areas. Culture was woven into every interaction, built naturally through connection and authenticity.

When the pandemic hit and operations were turned upside down, that culture held strong. It wasn't fragile because it wasn't fake. People didn't cling to policies; they clung to each other, to a leadership team that stayed present, honest, and anchored in love even when the future was uncertain. Leading is easy when things go smoothly; authentic leadership shines through in a crisis, where performative culture fades away, and only genuine connection remains.

When I consider why Dutch Bros. thrived while others struggled during the pandemic, it's not just because they had a more polished brand or better coffee *(though it's quite impressive)*; it's also because their leaders never lost sight of *who* they were serving. They understood culture is the engine that powers everything.

"Love is what we serve; coffee is the vessel we use to deliver it." –Travis Boersma, Co-Founder of Dutch Bros (Entrepreneur · Culture Builder · Champion of People)

Why Love-Based Leadership Is the Ultimate Competitive Advantage

In today's marketplace, almost anything can be copied. Competitors can imitate your pricing, menu, marketing, and even your technology. What they cannot duplicate is the emotional connection that arises from an authentic culture, one that is lived and fiercely protected. That's why love-based leadership offers a resilient advantage; it connects people to something greater than just a paycheck. When you lead with love, you build a company that customers can feel, even if they can't put it into words.

That's why culture isn't just a "soft skill"; it's a strategic asset. It gives your values practical expression, allowing people to experience them in ways a business plan never could. A strong culture turns employees into ambassadors, casual customers into loyal advocates, and ordinary transactions into lasting relationships. In the end, people commit to teams and organizations they believe in—and culture is the framework that allows that belief to scale.

So, what does this look like on a day-to-day basis?

Open Communication:
In many companies, information is kept on a "need-to-know" basis, which breeds distrust. In a people-first culture, communication is open, transparent, and frequent. Regular updates on how the business is truly performing, town-hall Q&As, and a culture of asking honest questions and providing honest answers foster loyalty within the team. Transparency doesn't mean revealing every confidential detail; it means respecting people enough to keep them informed. Trust is built through consistent dialogue, not surprise announcements.

Practice Daily Recognition:
In a love-based culture, appreciation comes naturally, not only through formal programs but also through simple, genuine moments: a quick "thank you" after a tough meeting, a public shout-out on Friday, or a handwritten note after a complex project. These moments don't just boost morale; they demonstrate that effort is recognized and valued. When people feel part of something big, they bring more of themselves to the work.

Invest in Growth:
Caring about development means funding courses, creating mentorships, and offering challenging assignments that allow people to learn in real time. Growth isn't just about promotions; it's about showing employees their future matters just as much as their current performance. A culture that invests in people retains talent longer and boosts the organization's capability.

Protect the Joy:
Don't overlook moments of fun. Laughter and shared joy serve as the social glue for high-performing teams. A quick trivia game, birthday celebrations, or a light-hearted contest can humanize the workplace and help teams better navigate challenges than working through everything alone.

Policies Communicate Values:
Flexible hours for parents, support for mental health days, and generous family leave all clearly convey the message, "We value you as a person, not just a worker." Culture isn't built by the words that are spoken but by what a company chooses to invest in, protect, and prioritize when setting rules.

These have been essential concepts in the way I have led throughout my entire career, especially protecting the joy. Work doesn't have to be a grind, and in those moments where it is, levity can cut through the tension to allow your team to breathe and refocus on the task at hand. Most jobs in any industry are not those that save lives daily; they are profit centers. Keep that in perspective!

An inconsistent culture will develop fractures, allowing resentment to grow. A consistent, love-based culture creates the conditions for people and performance to thrive. It doesn't require huge budgets; it demands intention, daily discipline, and leaders who embody the values they promote. That's how you retain great people and elevate the work. In the chapters ahead, you will also find that this will drive profits.

Leaders as Cultural Architects

Culture isn't something you delegate to HR, and you hope for the best. It starts with the people you choose to bring into the organization. You can hire the top-tier candidate with the Ivy League résumé and poor emotional intelligence, or the team player who may not check every box but exemplifies your brand's values. Some roles may require elite credentials (such as attorneys and CPAs), but more often, the so-called "B-player" thrives in the right culture, rising higher than anyone expected because they are aligned with the mission.

The best leaders I've worked with don't just establish cultural expectations during orientation but live by them every day. They personally attend new hire meetings because they grasp the importance of making a strong first impression. When a top performer's attitude endangers the team, they are the quickest to intervene and set things right. Metrics alone never justify toxic behavior. These leaders defend the culture with the same passionate energy they use to safeguard profits because they know that, in the long run, the two are interconnected.

The higher you move in the organization, the greater the impact of your actions. People don't just listen to what you say, they observe what you do, especially when you think no one's watching. If you value transparency but make big decisions behind closed doors or preach work-life balance but send midnight emails expecting quick replies or talk about teamwork while promoting lone wolves who don't collaborate, it sends a message. In culture, there is no neutral ground. Every action either reinforces or undermines your values. That's why leading by example is essential for building a strong culture.

Cultural architects safeguard the core values, which sometimes requires having tough conversations or even letting go of people who don't align with your brand. They may not be bad individuals, but their values conflict with what you're creating. Companies can lose their cultural integrity by tolerating a high-performing but toxic leader. Every time a bad fit is allowed to remain, hope diminishes. Every time leadership hesitates to act, cynicism increases. The most difficult decisions, especially about who stays and who leaves, reveal the true culture of your business.

The 'quiet heroes' are the people who live your values daily, and you may need to look past the loud achievers to see their worth within your organization. It's easy to reward the person who shines in the spotlight, but an authentic culture is revealed when you stop and recognize the one who lifts others without needing credit. It will be revealed when you promote the team player who brings people together or acknowledge someone who solves problems humbly and consistently. These moments send a message to the entire team about how people show up every day. The leader's job is to ensure that the right behaviors are noticed, reinforced, and repeated until they become the standard.

At its core, leadership isn't about controlling people. It's about creating an environment where individuals' best qualities can develop naturally. When you deliberately build that kind of environment, brick by brick, you're not just leading a company, you're cultivating a community and shaping a culture that will outlive you. A healthy culture is the lasting impact of leadership on the world, the kind of environment you leave behind when you're gone.

Real leadership doesn't lead from above; it lifts from within.

Measuring What Matters

There's an old saying in business: *"What gets measured gets managed."* However, in most companies, the only things measured are sales figures, expense reports, and quarterly targets. Culture, the invisible force that makes or breaks everything, is too often left to chance.

If you want a love-based, people-first culture to thrive, you have to take it as seriously as any financial KPI. That means measuring it, tending to it, and holding yourself accountable for its growth. Culture isn't static; it's a reflection of your daily choices as a leader, and it grows only where you choose to invest. It either becomes stronger with care and attention or, left unmanaged, it drifts into something you never intended. Love may be the determining factor that supports your most significant ROI. But if culture truly drives performance, then the question becomes: how do you measure something that feels intangible?

You start with engagement.

Engagement surveys, when conducted effectively, can provide valuable insights into whether your employees feel valued, trusted, and heard. But it's not about chasing high scores for the sake of bragging rights. It's about uncovering the real stories behind the numbers. Are some teams more connected than others? Are specific locations facing challenges? Where are trust levels strong, and where are they beginning to decline? Numbers are not the finish line; they are the entry point into honest conversations about how people are experiencing your culture.

Don't just conduct a survey once a year and then forget the results. Make culture metrics a genuine part of leadership conversations. When examining turnover rates, focus on the overall number, but also investigate regrettable attrition. Losing an underperformer might benefit the culture. But losing a beloved team builder? That's a five-alarm fire you need to explore. When you track culture with the same rigor as financials, you send a clear message: people aren't just part of the business—they are the business.

Other key indicators of a healthy culture include internal promotion rates, participation in professional development programs, and simple measures like how often peers recognize each other's work. Are people thanking one another without being prompted? That's a sign your culture isn't just top-down, but a living organism.

Make feedback loops two-way; don't just gather data from employees, but act on it. If survey results indicate a need for improvement in communication, avoid simply sending a memo stating, "We hear you!" and moving on. Demonstrate your responsiveness by scheduling additional town halls, launching a leadership blog, or establishing a Q&A channel. Whatever fits your organization. Make it clear that you listened and are changing your approach because you care about the well-being of your team.

One of my favorite examples of culture in action comes from companies that not only collect feedback but also act on it.

- At Adobe, concerns over outdated annual reviews led to a shift toward more frequent check-ins and the creation of space for improved dialogue and development.

- Atlassian *(a global software company best known for collaboration tools like Jira, Confluence, and Trello)* went even further by co-designing its career frameworks with input from employees, making sure those most affected had a say in shaping what growth could look like.[5]

- Even Google shaped its career development opportunities through structured feedback loops and peer input to help refine the system over time.[6]

In each case, the shift wasn't just about improving communication; it was about co-creation. When employees are involved in the process, the outcome is not only a more straightforward path but also a deeper sense of responsibility and ownership within the culture itself.

Not every great culture is born from feedback frameworks or tech-driven systems, though. Some, like In-N-Out, prove that

---

[5] Atlassian. "Do Operating Rhythms Drive Company Culture?" Work Check Podcast, Atlassian, 2022. https://www.atlassian.com/blog/podcast/work-check/season/season-1/do-operating-rhythms-drive-company-culture

[6] Garvin, D. A. How Google sold its engineers on management. Harvard Business Review, 91(12), 74–82. Harvard Business Review, December, 2013. https://hbr.org/2013/12/how-google-sold-its-engineers-on-management; re:Work with Google. Give feedback to managers. (Google's semi-annual manager feedback survey and process.)Rework.https://rework.withgoogle.com/intl/en/guides/managers-give-feedback-to-managers; Bock, L. Work rules!: Insights from inside Google that will transform how you live and lead. Twelve, 2015.

simplicity, values, and consistency can be just as influential in shaping a thriving culture.

Driving Culture with Purpose and Personality

The culture at In-N-Out is both purposeful and distinctive. The brand's limited menu and decision to remain private reflect a commitment to quality over scale. Lynsi Snyder (CEO) promotes a culture focused on family, faith, and service, with Christian values still reflected in their packaging and philanthropic efforts.

SmartBrief highlighted the company's focus on respect, transparency, and manager-led engagement, noting that "great managers are In-N-Out's secret sauce". On the operational side, maintaining fresh, in-house food and clean, bright stores reinforces their brand standards. Ultimately, aside from the relaxed uniforms and simple menus, the brand's real secret is its values-driven employee strategy: hire well, treat people like family, train them thoroughly, promote from within, and build a culture that's authentic, scalable, and human at its core.[7] The result is employees who take pride in the mission of In-N-Out.

If In-N-Out embodies culture through disciplined simplicity and values-driven operations, Trader Joe's expresses it through curated discovery and a sense of neighborhood warmth. The methods may differ, but the effect is unmistakable: people don't just see the culture, but they experience it.

---

[7] Edmonds, S. C. 3 takeaways from In-N-Out Burger's work culture. SmartBrief, March 26, 2024. https://www.smartbrief.com/original/3-takeaways-from-in-n-out-burgers-work-culture; In-N-Out Burger. Food quality. https://www.in-n-out.com/menu/food-quality In-N-Out.com; In-N-Out Burger. Menu. https://www.in-n-out.com/menu In-N-Out.com; In-N-Out Burger. Media kit [Press information]. https://www.in-n-out.com/mediakit/

Joe Coulombe intentionally built a company that felt like a quirky, neighborhood escape. Stores weren't meant to mimic big-box efficiency; they were designed to feel like a mix between a tropical outpost and a local market. The Fearless Flyer newsletter, tropical uniforms, and hand-crafted signage reinforced a brand identity rooted in discovery, storytelling, and human connection. At Trader Joe's, culture isn't a byproduct; it is the product.

But it wasn't just about appearances. Trader Joe's also distinguished itself with a curated product mix built around the needs and desires of its core customer: the "overeducated and underpaid." Coulombe believed in intensive buying, selecting fewer products but choosing them with care. That same intentionality extended to how the business was run. Coulombe believed in complete transparency with staff, sharing store financials and company strategy to foster better understanding and alignment. Employees were encouraged to learn about the products and serve as helpful guides, rather than pushy salespeople.

Most importantly, the culture was fun. Staff were empowered to bring creativity to their roles. Many doubled as artists, writers, or local personalities within their stores. With strong compensation, autonomy, and a clear sense of purpose, Trader Joe's created a culture that is both high-performing and unmistakably people-centered.

You can't fake that level of authenticity, and you definitely can't buy it either. You earn it by listening, responding, and making culture measurement a shared responsibility.

The truth is that your culture is always communicating. Whether it's how meetings feel, the stories employees share, or the small everyday interactions that no leadership memo will ever capture.

The only question is: Are you listening?

The Take-a-Way

Just like a great gardener doesn't just measure the harvest but tends the soil, leaders who care about culture aren't obsessed with outcomes alone. They're obsessed with the health of the environment that produces those outcomes.

Culture is the soil from which everything else grows.
If you nurture it daily, the fruits will take care of themselves.

CHAPTER 5

Choose Your Culture Before It Chooses You

"Treat a man as he is and he will remain as he is. Treat a man as he can and should be, and he will become as he can and should be."

–Johann Wolfgang von Goethe
(August 1749–March 22, 1832)

The Trea Turner Story: How Community and Culture Created a Superstar

Before donning a Phillies uniform, Trea Turner had already built a reputation as one of baseball's most electrifying players. A two-time All-Star and World Series champion with the Washington Nationals, Turner brought a rare mix of elite speed, gold-glove defense, and consistent offensive production. After a strong stint with the Los Angeles Dodgers, he entered free agency as one of the most coveted players in the league. The Philadelphia Phillies made a bold move, signing him to an eleven-year, $300 million contract that came with expectations as high as the price tag.

But reality rarely follows the script.

As the 2023 season began, Turner struggled mightily. Through 107 games, he was hitting .235 with a .658 OPS, well below his usual standard. On August 2, in Miami, he went hitless in five at-bats and committed a costly fielding error that sealed a Phillies loss. For a city known for both its loyalty and intensity, the frustration was palpable. Philadelphia fans don't sugarcoat their feelings, and by the time the team returned home, Turner was bracing for the boos.

Then something remarkable happened.

A local fan known as "The Philly Captain," John McCann, took to social media, not to pile on, but to rally support. He urged fans to show compassion instead of criticism. When Turner stepped to the plate on August 4, instead of boos, he was met with a thunderous standing ovation. The stadium roared in unison, loud, spontaneous, and full of heart.

It was a simple gesture, but one that cut through the noise. You could see it hit him. Turner, visibly emotional, tipped *his helmet, took a breath, and something shifted. From that moment on, his season underwent a transformation. He found his rhythm again, finishing the year with twenty-six home runs and leading the Phillies deep into the postseason. The slump was over, but more importantly, something deeper had been restored: belief.*

Philadelphia had done what few organizations in any field remember to do: they chose grace over judgment. That single act of empathy reignited a superstar and redefined a season.

Trea Turner's comeback wasn't just about rediscovering his swing; it was about rediscovering connection. In a city known for its grit, fans showed the world another kind of strength, the courage to believe in someone when it's hardest. That's what culture looks like in action. One act of collective kindness turned pressure into purpose.

In business, our "standing ovations" come in different forms: recognition, encouragement, conviction, and daily signals that say, we're with you. It's those moments that convert potential into performance. What happened in Philadelphia wasn't a fluke; it was culture doing its job in the public eye. When belief becomes visible, performance follows. The same principle is true in every workplace: people rise when they know they're seen, supported, and believed in.

NOTE: *Psychologists have noted that the presence of an audience creates a phenomenon known as "social facilitation," where individuals' performance changes when others are present.*

Choosing the Culture That Inspires Your Team

So how do you build a culture that energizes your business rather than exhausts it, one that grows without losing its essence, where people feel safe and motivated every day? This chapter is about that quest. It's what businesses learn through trial, error, and a few hard lessons. It's about creating a place people genuinely want to belong.

Culture doesn't wait for you to figure it out. It shows up whether you're ready or not. The big question is: Did you choose it, or did it choose you?

Ever walked into a place and felt your shoulders tighten before you even reached the front desk? The air feels heavy, the greeting absent, and the space is more closed off than welcoming. It's as if the room itself were allergic to joy, and once you sense it in a workplace, it's hard to shake.

Most of the time, bad culture isn't one giant mistake: it's a slow leak. It's little comments that go unchecked, a toxic leader, and missed appreciation; these can manifest in many forms. They are typically small, but over time, the low hum grows louder, like a lion's roar, until it becomes impossible to ignore. And before you know it, you look up and realize, "Uh oh. We built something. But this isn't it."

But the opposite is just as tangible. There are places where you exhale the second you walk in. The energy is warm, the smiles are genuine, and even the smallest gestures make you feel welcome. In these spaces, culture isn't left to chance; it's the product of deliberate choices. The best brands are aware of this and design with intention.

A positive workplace culture is rooted in shared values, genuine care for people, and a relentless commitment to service. Companies like Chick-fil-A, Trader Joe's, Zappos, and Costco consistently set themselves apart by prioritizing people over profits:

- Chick-fil-A is known for both its efficiency and the warmth and courtesy of its team members, who are empowered to go the extra mile. They provide clear expectations, training, and confidence to their team, which results in consistently high service across thousands of locations.[8]

- Trader Joe's thrives on friendliness and authenticity, creating a neighborhood-store feel where employees are empowered to meaningfully engage with their customers. The culture fosters an environment centered on presence, helpfulness, and autonomy at the store level, enhancing both team morale and long-term customer loyalty.[9]

- Zappos built its entire business model around a customer-first philosophy, driven by a culture of fun, conviction, and employee autonomy. Culture is integrated into the hiring process, leadership development, and customer service philosophy, creating alignment between values and behavior.[10]

---

[8] Lynch, Brooke. "Why Chick-Fil-A Employees Deliver Outstanding Customer Service | CCW Digital." CCW Digital, November 21, 2024. https://www.customercontactweekdigital.com/ccw-analyst-insights/articles/chick-fil-a-employee-experience; Triplett, Angela. "4 Lessons in Employee Empowerment Courtesy of Chick-Fil-A." Customer Service Profiles LLC, November 2, 2016. https://www.csp.com/chick-fil-a.
[9] Emmer, Marc. "How Trader Joe's Built an Iconic Brand through Employee Engagement." Inc.com, January 13, 2020. https://www.inc.com/marc-emmer/how-trader-joes-built-an-iconic-brand-through-employee-engagement.html; Johnson, Greg. "Trader Joe's: A Different Culture." Blue Book, March 19, 2021. https://www.bluebookservices.com/trader-joes-a-different-culture; Petrak, Lynn. "Yes, Being Nice Is a Thing at Trader Joe's." Progressive Grocer, August 9, 2024. https://progressivegrocer.com/yes-being-nice-thing-trader-joes.
[10] Digitopia. "Zappos' Culture of Delivering Happiness: Putting Employees First for Exceptional Customer Service - Digitopia," October 3, 2024. https://digitopia.co/blog/zappos-culture; Renascence.io. "What Makes Zappos a Leader in Customer Experience (CX)?," 2023. https://

- Costco stands out for how well it treats both its customers and employees, offering competitive wages, long-term growth opportunities, and a sense of belonging that's rare in retail. Their approach of promoting people from within helps to maintain a low-turnover workforce, demonstrating that investing in people directly improves operational performance.[11]

What makes these companies different is that culture isn't an afterthought; it's their foundation. They don't just hire for skill; they hire for attitude, invest in training, and foster environments where people feel respected, seen, and inspired to deliver their best.

Other brands such as Salesforce, Patagonia, and Southwest Airlines provide further evidence that culture is a long-term asset:

- Salesforce embeds values like care and inclusion into business operations, from how they measure success to how leaders communicate with their teams.[12]

---

www.renascence.io/journal/what-makes-zappos-a-leader-in-customer-experience-cx; Titus Talent Strategies. "Zappos: A Case Study into Company Culture | Titus Talent Strategies." Titus Talent Strategies, September 12, 2023. https://www.titustalent.com/insights/zappos-a-case-study-into-company-culture.

[11] Perman, Cindy. "Costco and Other Retailers Prove a 'Good Jobs' Strategy Works." Harvard Business School, December 3, 2024. https://www.hbs.edu/bigs/costco-and-other-retailers-prove-a-good-jobs-strategy-works; Relihan, Tom. "How Costco's Obsession with Culture Drove Success." MIT Sloan, May 11, 2018. https://mitsloan.mit.edu/ideas-made-to-matter/how-costcos-obsession-culture-drove-success.

[12] Salesforce. "Our Values Guide Every Decision," 2022. https://www.salesforce.com/company/our-values; Salesforce. "Purpose-Driven Culture, Powered by People," 2022. https://www.salesforce.com/company/careers/culture; trailhead.salesforce.com. "Explore Salesforce Culture and Values," n.d. https://trailhead.salesforce.com/content/

- Patagonia reinforces its purpose through hiring, product design, and activism, giving employees a clear connection between their work and the company's larger mission.[13]

- Southwest Airlines, known for its operational efficiency, has long prioritized team cohesion and transparent communication as essential to delivering consistent performance under pressure.[14]

These companies stand out from their competitors because they emphasize disciplined, value-driven leadership. They clearly communicate what matters, reinforce it through structure and behavior, and create accountability around it. In such environments, culture becomes more than just an idea; it evolves into a system that enhances retention, accelerates decision-making, and enhances the customer experience.

learn/modules/salesforce-culture-and-values/explore-salesforce -culture-and-values.

[13] Culture Amp. "Patagonia's Vincent Stanley on Creating a Purpose-Driven Work Culture | Culture Amp," October 22, 2024. https://www.cultureamp.com/podcast/patagonia; CultureMonkey. "Patagonia Company Culture in Action: How HR Can Apply These Values Anywhere," July 24, 2025. https://www.culturemonkey.io/employee-engagement/patagonia-company-culture/; Patagonia Careers. "Careers at Patagonia | Patagonia Jobs," 2024. https://careers.patagonia.com/us/en/; Patagonia Employee Benefits. "Empowering through Activism and Civic Engagement," 2025. https://careers.patagonia.com/us/en/benefits.https://careers.patagonia.com/us/en/benefits.

[14] Brown, Lisa. "Southwest Airlines Co.'S Organizational Culture & Its Characteristics: An Analysis." Panmore Institute, May 14, 2019. https://panmore.com/southwest-airlines-co-organizational-culture-characteristics-analysis; Elite Team Tactics. "How Southwest Airlines Built a High-Performance Culture," 2025. https://www.eliteteamtactics.com/p/how-southwest-airlines-built-a-high-performance-culture-1dbe; Southwest Airlines. "Our People and Culture | Southwest Airlines." www.southwest.com, 2025. https://www.southwest.com/citizenship/people/.

When executed effectively, a positive culture becomes the core way the business operates.

Building from the Core: Culture Before Everything

"Culture isn't just one aspect of the game—it is the game."
—Louis V. Gerstner Jr., Former IBM CEO

The heartbeat of every organization begins long before the first product launch or hire. It's found in the values that shape decisions, the integrity behind small choices, and the way leaders show up every day. That's what forms culture, the foundation on which everything else stands. The best time to define it is before the first employee walks through the door. The next best time? Right now.

Excellence doesn't emerge by accident; it grows through intention. When a leader is honest enough to say, *"This isn't working,"* that's the moment transformation begins. Cultures don't crumble overnight; they erode through neglect, inconsistency, and silence. Whether you're scaling rapidly, rebuilding after loss, or aligning a divided team, growth will always test your foundation. A business can only expand as far as its culture is willing to stretch.

Alignment starts where conviction meets consistency; it's a visible behavior. How you open meetings, recognize effort, or confront missed expectations all tell a story louder than any mission statement. People respond to patterns they can trust. What you tolerate teaches just as powerfully as what you celebrate.

When I interviewed with Greg Semos for my final round at McDonald's in 2003, he told me something that still defines how I view leadership: *"Our real product isn't burgers—it's people."* McDonald's didn't choose franchisees or managers solely based on operational expertise; instead, it chose those who aligned with its culture. He spoke about *Hamburger*

University, McDonald's global leadership center that served as both a classroom and a cultural compass.

Over 275,000 people have graduated from *Hamburger University*, with programs accredited by the American Council on Education. Managers can earn up to 23 college credits, which are transferable to hundreds of U.S. schools. That's not training; it's a declaration that says, 'We believe in you enough to invest in your future.'

Even with fierce competitors like Burger King, Wendy's, and Chick-fil-A, McDonald's advantage wasn't size; it was its ability to *teach* culture. Through *Hamburger University*, it codified the values, rituals, and expectations that define its brand so clearly that a store in Tokyo could feel as familiar as one in Chicago or São Paulo.

That's how culture scales, by teaching it, not preaching it. Strategy may fuel growth, but culture sustains it.

Lead the Culture or It Will Lead You

You can sense a company's culture, even if you can't always name it. When it's off, everyone takes notice. A culture that is not intentionally designed often leads to dysfunction. Silos form, cliques develop, and the ego begins to overshadow collaboration. Turnover naturally increases because people leave environments that drain them. Top performers quietly exit, while average employees do just enough to get by. Most importantly, customers can feel it because culture is always customer-facing, whether you realize it or not. If you do not actively shape your company's culture, it will drift, and often it won't move in the right direction.

That's why it's essential to consider the other side of the equation. Just as strong cultures can drive long-term success, toxic or misaligned cultures can lead to decline or even collapse. History is full of companies that looked invincible on the outside but were corroded on the inside. Here are a few well-documented examples of companies whose culture directly contributed to their downfall:

1. **Enron – Culture of Deception and Greed**
   Enron is perhaps the most infamous example of cultural failure. The company's leadership created a high-pressure, hyper-competitive environment where employees were rewarded for aggressive risk-taking and discouraged from being transparent. The culture prioritized short-term gains over ethics and accountability, ultimately fostering widespread financial fraud. Executives manipulated earnings to inflate stock prices, and employees who questioned these practices were silenced or ignored. When the fraud was uncovered, Enron collapsed in one of the largest corporate scandals in U.S. history. The failure was not only technical but also cultural in nature.[15]

   Update: *Enron did not rehabilitate itself—it filed for Chapter 11 on Dec. 2, 2001, and was wound down rather than restructured (History.com)[16]. Its estate operated as Enron Creditors Recovery Corp., pursuing lawsuits and settlements that ultimately returned about $21.8–$23 billion to creditors, before the entity was dissolved in 2016 (Reuters; Wikipedia).[17] The scandal also resulted in criminal convictions of senior executives and contributed to the passage of the Sarbanes-Oxley Act of 2002, which tightened corporate reporting and auditing oversight (FBI; Britannica).[18]*

2. **Uber (Pre-2017) – Toxic, Aggressive, and Unchecked**
   Uber's early success was overshadowed by a deeply flawed internal culture that prioritized rapid growth over ethical behavior. Under founder Travis Kalanick, the company gained a reputation for employing aggressive tactics, lacking accountability, and tolerating harassment and discrimination. A viral blog post by

a former employee in 2017 detailed systemic sexism and HR negligence, sparking an internal investigation. The culture, described by many insiders as toxic and combative, led to multiple executive departures, brand damage, and eventually Kalanick's resignation. Uber didn't fail as a company, but its unchecked culture severely damaged its reputation, delayed its IPO, and necessitated a full-scale cultural overhaul.[15]

Update: After Susan Fowler's 2017 exposé exposed deep-seated sexism and broken HR processes, Uber brought in former U.S. Attorney General Eric Holder to investigate (Vanity Fair, 2017).[16] That investigation initiated sweeping cultural reforms. In 2018, new CEO Dara Khosrowshahi emphasized transparency and ethics, establishing the core value, "We do the right thing. Period." He also reshaped leadership and enforced accountability throughout the organization (New Yorker, 2018).[17] These changes marked the beginning of Uber's lengthy, yet deliberate, cultural turnaround.

3. Wells Fargo – Performance at Any Cost
Wells Fargo's fake accounts scandal exemplifies a company whose internal culture directly led to failure. Employees, pressured to meet unrealistic sales targets, opened millions of unauthorized bank accounts to reach quotas. The culture rewarded aggressive sales tactics and punished those who didn't comply, creating an environment where ethical boundaries were often crossed. Leadership initially denied responsibility, and accountability was slow to emerge. The fallout included billions in fines, loss of customer confidence, and executive resignations. The root cause? A culture that focused on performance without ethics.[15]

Update: In June 2025, the Federal Reserve lifted the growth cap it had imposed in 2018, acknowledging Wells Fargo's cultural and governance reforms. Under

CEO Charlie Scharf, the bank restructured its leadership, strengthened compliance and risk management, and recognized employees with a $2,000 bonus for their contributions to the turnaround (Associated Press, 2025; Reuters, 2025).[16]

4. WeWork – Charisma over Competence

WeWork, once valued at nearly $50 billion, experienced a dramatic crash in 2019 following its failed IPO. Founder Adam Neumann fostered a cult-like culture that was characterized by overconfidence, self-promotion, and blurred lines between personal and professional decision-making. The company expanded hastily, making large real estate commitments without a solid business model. Internally, the culture lacked transparency, proper governance, and financial discipline. Visionary branding masked reckless leadership, and unchecked ego ultimately led to the brand's downfall, resulting in billions of dollars in lost investor value. The company survived, but its valuation dropped sharply, and its founder was forced out. Culture wasn't a minor issue; it was the core problem.[15]

Update: *WeWork emerged from bankruptcy in 2024 after eliminating $4 billion in debt and closing more than 160 unprofitable leases. With John Santora appointed as CEO, the company shifted toward financial discipline and stability, eventually reporting positive EBITDA in 2025, marking a significant recovery (Time, 2025; Wikipedia, 2025).*[16]

5. Theranos – Secrecy, Fear, and False Promises

Theranos, led by Elizabeth Holmes, fostered a culture of secrecy and fear where dissent was punished and the truth was suppressed. Employees were discouraged from asking questions, siloed to prevent collaboration, and often fired for raising concerns. The internal culture prioritized appearances over facts, leading to years of deception about the capabilities of its blood-testing technology. Ultimately, the truth emerged, the technology was proven to be fraudulent, and the company collapsed. Like Enron, Theranos didn't fail because of a bad idea—it failed because its culture made it impossible to confront the truth.[15]

Update: *Theranos ultimately failed to recover and dissolved in 2018 after investigations uncovered massive fraud and regulatory violations (Investopedia; Wikipedia).[16] Its founder, Elizabeth Holmes, was convicted in 2022 for defrauding investors and received a prison sentence of over eleven years. An appeals court confirmed that decision in early 2025 (ABC News).[17] The company no longer exists, and its legacy is more of a cautionary tale than a success story.*

In each of these instances, flawed culture was the primary driver behind poor decisions, ethical mistakes, and leadership failures. When culture goes unchecked, when performance is prioritized over people, or when dissent is suppressed, even the most promising companies can collapse. The lesson is clear: you can't outgrow or outscale a broken culture; it will eventually catch up with you.

Leadership's role will be to rebuild trust, reshape values, and demonstrate that course correction is possible. That's the key component to remember: culture is not a finished product; it's a living entity. It can drift, break, and heal. Humility, accountability, and a willingness to change can turn even the most severe cautionary tale into a story of redemption.

Culture Is Oxygen to Your Brand

Culture should be like oxygen: essential, invisible, and life-sustaining. Without it, people might function for a while, but eventually, they begin to suffocate. When deliberately designed, it becomes a sustainable way to influence how people think, act, and connect. When it's absent, morale erodes, decisions slow, and your best people quietly leave in search of clarity, purpose, and connection.

And if I may channel a little classic rock wisdom here:

> **"Love is like oxygen...you get too much, you get too high. Not enough and you're gonna die."**
> —Sweet, 1978

The same principle applies to culture. Too much of the wrong thing, like ego, control, and ambiguity, and you lose sight of what truly matters. A lack of culture makes an organization unsustainable. An effective culture finds the right balance, and when you succeed in creating one that is authentic, balanced, and rooted in shared values, it creates something special.

A strong culture shows people how to contribute, lead, and face challenges with confidence. It creates consistency in decisions and unites teams around a common purpose, and doesn't just elevate the good days; it steadies the hard ones. At its core, it's about shared standards, mutual respect, and accountability, which foster a supportive and cohesive environment.

Ego can undermine all of this. If left unchecked, it creates distance between leaders and their teams, distorts communication, promotes self-interest, and erodes the culture that it was meant to protect. A healthy culture does the opposite: it respects authority but isn't afraid to challenge it, asks tough questions, and demands accountability. Where culture brings clarity and cohesion, ego breeds confusion and division. When *ego* wins, organizations fracture; but when *culture* prevails, they endure.

Just like oxygen, culture is easy to overlook when it's present, but impossible to ignore when it's absent. It is the stabilizer of every system, fueling clarity, resilience, and long-term protection. Ultimately, culture isn't a performance accessory; it's the air an organization breathes. And the question every leader must ask is simple: Are you giving your people the oxygen they need to thrive?

Why We Cheer Louder When It's Personal

Mark, David, and Ethan sat high in the Olympic stadium, hot dogs in hand, soaked in the crackling energy of the finals. They were in Paris, on a long-planned trip, ready to cheer for their country.

"Next up, the 1500-meter final," the announcer boomed. "For the home team… number 124, Jean-Luc Fournier!"

Mark nudged Ethan: "That's the same last name as David."

David looked up. "Fournier? No way."

On the jumbotron: **F O U R N I E R**–spelled exactly like his. From that moment, the race became personal. It wasn't just a contest; it was theirs, too.

"Let's go, Fournier!" David yelled, and Mark and Ethan roared with him. They tracked every stride. Fournier was boxed in at fourth as the bell rang. The crowd's roar grew, but theirs rose above it.

"Push it, **FOURNIER!**" Mark shouted.

Something unlocked. He surged forward, breaking free of the pack. In the final straightaway, he overtook second place just as they crossed the line–silver medal. The stadium erupted. The three friends hugged tight, proud, stunned.

"Did you see that? Our guy did it!" David cried.

Later, in a Paris pub, they relived the race. The shared name was silly, but it gave them a connection. Their cheers weren't just support: they were ownership. That strange tie made the triumph feel as if it belonged to them.

It was a reminder that when we lean in, even the smallest link can transform a moment into something unforgettable. That's what culture does inside organizations, too: it turns effort into ownership and work into something people are proud to claim as their own.

CHAPTER 6

The Legacy You Leave Behind

"Carve your name on hearts, not tombstones. A legacy is etched into the minds of others and the stories they share about you."

–Shannon L. Alder

Permission to Care

On March 18, 2016, at the Dutch Bros. Coffee on Northeast 138th Avenue in Vancouver, Washington, a moment unfolded that would resonate far beyond the confines of the coffee stand. A woman, visibly distraught, pulled up to the window. She had just lost her thirty-seven-year-old husband the night before and was overwhelmed with grief. Recognizing her anguish, employees Evan Freeman, Peirce Dunn, and Jacob Hancock paused their routine to offer solace. They engaged her in conversation, extended a free coffee, and, most notably, reached out through the drive-thru window to hold her hand in prayer.

This heartfelt interaction was captured by customer Barbara Danner, who was in line behind the grieving woman. She shared the photo on Facebook, noting how the Dutch Bros. staff "stopped everything and prayed with her for several minutes." The image quickly went viral, amassing over 197,500 likes and more than 64,800 shares within days.

Jessica Chudek, owner of that Dutch Bros. location, expressed her pride in her employees' actions, saying, "We encourage them to pour love out of that window in whatever way is comfortable for them." This incident not only highlighted the compassion of the Dutch Bros. team but also underscored the profound impact of genuine human connection in moments of despair.

Moments like the one at Dutch Bros. aren't scripted; they stem from a culture that empowers people to be themselves. When leaders allow their teams permission to lead with heart, to act with authenticity, and to treat others with kindness, the results go far beyond productivity. They foster connections, loyalty, and a sense of purpose. That day in the drive-thru, those employees didn't just serve coffee; they served humanity. And they did it because the culture supported it. When you create a workplace where love, individuality, and *purpose are not only accepted but encouraged, culture stops being just a concept and becomes a living expression of who you are. That's the kind of culture people remember. That's the kind of culture that endures. One of the Broistas commented, "This was nothing special; this is what we do every day."*

Leadership

Culture depends on strong leaders. Leadership isn't just about the present; it's about what you leave behind once you're no longer in control. Culture needs to be built for the long term, ensuring that even after you're gone, the values you practiced continue to influence decisions.

The truth is simple but profound: your legacy is the culture you created.

Not the buildings you built, the awards on your wall, or the revenue milestones. It's how you made people feel, how you shaped their careers, how you helped them become better versions of themselves.

That's the Real Scoreboard!

At Dutch Bros, the vibrant culture rooted in love isn't just a concept; it's something you can truly see, hear, and feel every day. It comes alive in how people greet one another, how leaders listen attentively, and how decisions are made with purpose and intention. The open seating during lunch, the absence of closed-door meetings, and the Friday "Dub Shots" aren't just fun perks; they are intentional choices that promote openness and a shared sense of ownership. These small but meaningful details quietly say, 'You really matter here.' Every operator, trainer, and Broista knows they're not just completing tasks but helping craft an experience and caring for something bigger than themselves.

Cultures rooted in growth and respect outlast leaders, markets, and metrics. That's more than just branding; that's legacy in action.

"Let all that you do be done in love." –1 Corinthians 16:14

What You Build Is Who You Are

"Not all of us can do great things. But we can do small things with great love."

–Mother Teresa

Every policy, hire, and performance review is a thread in the tapestry of culture you are weaving. Over time, those threads interlock into a design that either inspires pride or reveals flaws for everyone to see. With each decision, leaders must ask themselves: Am I weaving something I'd be proud to see displayed as part of my legacy? It's easy to prioritize speed over standards or convenience over values, especially under pressure. But culture has a long memory. The frays caused by compromise, inconsistency, or fear-based leadership may not be immediately visible, but over time, they unravel clarity and cohesion.

This approach mirrors what great culture-driven companies understand. At Four Seasons, employee training goes far beyond following procedures—it empowers staff to anticipate guest needs and respond to them. Housekeepers may notice a guest prefers sleeping on the left side of the bed or always eats apples but avoids bananas. Staff are trained and trusted to act on these insights, placing slippers on the preferred side or restocking extra apples without being asked. That kind of anticipatory service stems from a culture that equips employees to "go beyond the call of duty," reinforcing luxury through intuitive, unprompted care (Meyer, 2011).[15]

At Chick-fil-A, every decision reflects a deeper value system, turning food into exceptional hospitality. The company's "culture of care" urges people to express themselves through phrases like "we're here to serve," "we're better together," and "we are purpose-driven." These phrases shape daily interactions with customers. They aren't just words; they set the tone for every interaction and sustain the integrity of the brand. Employees are trained to show genuine warmth and thoughtful touches, whether it's offering an unexpected napkin, refilling a drink, or sincerely saying "my pleasure." These details don't just serve the customer; they convey the brand's values. This value-driven approach makes each interaction special, redefining what service can be.[16]

Both companies understand that culture isn't about what you say, it's about the behavior you promote. When people consistently practice these principles, they do more than guide performance; they begin to shape identity. These activities are lived out regularly; they stop being just something you do and instead start influencing everything you do *next*.

That influence becomes most visible when the leader steps away. If culture unravels in your absence, or depends on your

---

[15] Meyer, K. Four Seasons: Our key competitive difference is our people. January 26, 2011. https://www.kevinmeyer.com/four-seasons-our-key-competitive-difference-is-our-people/

[16] Chick-fil-A. "Culture & Values." Chick-fil-A, 2025. https://www.chick-fil-a.com/careers/culture; Chick-fil-A. "What Are Chick-Fil-A's Core Values?" Chick-fil-A, 2025. https://www.chick-fil-a.com/customer-support/who-we-are/our-culture-and-values/what-are-chick-fil-a-core-values; Training Simplified. "The Secret Sauce behind Chick-Fil-A's World-Class Service." Training Simplified, January 21, 2025. https://www.trainingsimplified.com/blog/the-secret-sauce-behind-chick-fil-as-world-class-service.

personality, presence, or constant oversight, you haven't built a culture; you've built a dependency. True leadership is measured by how well the values endure without you. In practice, it means handing over decisions with confidence so others can carry them forward.

You must empower people to make decisions, lift young leaders, and encourage them to challenge legacy processes. A strong culture isn't fixed in place; responsibility evolves with time and people. But if it's built with intention, its DNA remains consistent: love, authenticity, and a commitment to excellence. The role of leadership is not to preserve culture in a frozen state, but to embed its values so profoundly that even as new people step in and the company grows, the essence of what made it great remains intact. If you do it right, your fingerprints will still be visible in the laughter in the break room, the collaboration in the team meetings, and the loyalty of customers who feel like part of the family.

That is leadership's true legacy—and the most important work you'll ever do.

Leaving a Legacy for the Next Generation

Some organizations go beyond growth and profit, choosing to anchor their culture in values that endure long after they are gone. Patagonia, for example, built a legacy rooted in environmental responsibility and employee empowerment. Even after founder Yvon Chouinard transferred ownership to a trust, the company's core values remained intact because they were embedded at every level.[17]

---

[17] Harvard Business Review. "What Happens When a Company (like Patagonia) Transfers Ownership to a Nonprofit?" Harvard Business Review, October 10, 2022. https://hbr.org/2022/10/what-happens-when-a-company-like-patagonia-becomes-a-nonprofit; Patagonia. "Earth Is Now Our Only Shareholder." www.patagonia.com. Patagonia, September 14, 2022. https://www.patagonia.com/ownership/.

The Ritz-Carlton's Gold Standards aren't just hospitality pro-tocols; they are cultural cornerstones. To this day, every employee, from housekeeping to executive leadership, is empowered to spend up to $2,000 to resolve a guest issue without managerial approval. That's culture codified into action.[18]

REI has taken an unusually bold step in retail: for more than a decade, it has closed all its stores on Black Friday, paying its thousands of employees to enjoy the outdoors instead, and encouraging customers to do the same, turning culture into action rather than just marketing. (REI Co-op Newsroom, 2024).[19]

HP, one of the original Silicon Valley companies, became known for the "HP Way," a culture built on conviction, respect, and decentralized decision-making. Rather than relying on top-down authority, leaders empowered engineers and teams to innovate, setting a standard for tech companies that followed.[20]

Netflix, best known for reinventing entertainment through streaming, has also reshaped corporate culture with its "Freedom & Responsibility" philosophy. By granting employ-ees broad autonomy and holding them to high standards of

---

[18] Renascence. "How the Ritz-Carlton Enhances Customer Experience (CX) through Personalized Service and Luxury." Renascence.io, 2024. https://www.renascence.io/journal/how-the-ritz-carlton-enhances-customer-experience-cx-through-personalized-service-and-luxury.
[19] REI. "REI Co-Op Continues Its Annual Black Friday Tradition, Closing Its Doors and Paying Employees to Opt Outside." REI, October 2, 2024. https://www.rei.com/newsroom/article/rei-co-op-continues-its-ann ual-black-friday-tradition-closing-its-doors-and-paying-employees-to-opt-outside.
[20] Hewlett-Packard Company. "The HP Way (internal report)." July 1977.

accountability, Netflix has created a culture where improvement thrives, and bureaucracy is minimized.[21]

IDEO, the global design firm behind products like Apple's first mouse, embeds creativity and collaboration into its DNA. With a flat structure and cross-disciplinary teams, IDEO encourages employees to experiment, fail fast, and co-create solutions, creating a culture where curiosity is not just encouraged but required.[22]

What unites these examples is that culture isn't treated as branding or a perk; it is operationalized into daily behaviors, policies, and choices that outlast the founders. Ultimately, culture is the lasting imprint you leave behind.

The question isn't whether your company will be remembered. The question is: *what will they be remembered for?*

Love, when wielded with wisdom, becomes a leader's most powerful strategy.

---

[21] Harvard Business School. "Netflix: A creative approach to culture and agility (Case No. 56185)." Harvard Business School Publishing.
[22] Amabile, T., Fisher, C. M., & Pillemer, J. "IDEO's culture of helping." Harvard Business Review. January–February 2014.

CHAPTER 7

The ROI of Culture

"To win in the marketplace, you must first win in the work-place."

–Doug Conant, former CEO of Campbell Soup Company

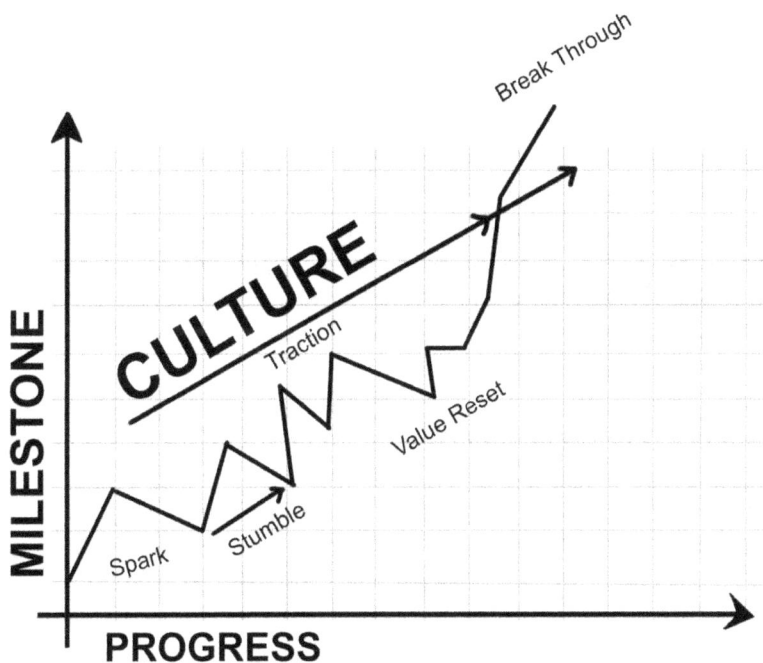

The Measure of a Leader: Grace over EGO

In 2004, I attended a CKE Restaurants corporate meeting in Las Vegas. What I didn't expect was that a brief elevator ride would leave me with a story I'd carry for decades. When the doors opened, I was stunned to find myself sharing an elevator ride with a celebrity. The most memorable part was his humility and the character of the man as we stood shoulder to shoulder, sharing a few moments together.

It was the morning of my departure from the Bellagio. I stepped into the elevator on the 29th floor, loaded down with two suitcases, a golf bag, and a box of conference materials. I was determined to make it in one trip. Around the 22nd floor, the doors opened, and a man entered who greeted me casually, then glanced at my awkward cargo and joked, "Traveling light, huh?" We laughed, and I told him I'd seen him perform at our company event the night before. "You crushed it," I said. "Not only are you a great musician, but your sense of humor had me in stitches." He thanked me and asked, "Was it really a good performance? You know you wonder sometimes." I replied, "No, really, it was awesome! The whole company was up and dancing, the women swooning, and the men rethinking their career decisions." We both laughed again.

We talked as the elevator descended. He wasn't rushed or distracted; he was present. When we reached the lobby, he held the door open as I tried to wrangle my gear. "Can I help you with that?" he asked. "Nah, I'm good, you have better things to do with your time," I said. He shrugged and said, "Before I started getting paid to play music, I worked in a hotel. Helped guests with bags every day. At night, they'd let me play in the lounge. That's where I met the guy who gave me my first real break."

He grabbed a couple of bags, and we walked together to the front desk, chatting like peers. I asked him how he ended up performing at our event. Apparently, the original artist–Alicia Keys, if I remember correctly–had fallen ill, and his father (also his agent) got the call. He had another show coming up, but took this one on short notice. "My dad said, 'Go do it. Always take the opportunity to perform," he said.

As we reached the front desk, the lobby was buzzing; a hundred or so friends, franchisees, and colleagues were checking out. I couldn't resist. Never one to stay quiet when a good moment presents itself, I turned to the crowd and said, "Hey, does every-one see who's carrying my bags? It's Gavin DeGraw!" Every head turned, and within minutes, Gavin was surrounded–signing autographs, taking photos, and sharing laughs as if he were part of the team.

Looking back, I could have been more discreet. But he handled it with grace, not ego. He hung out with people longer than he needed to, thanked everyone, and before heading out, hugged me and said, "Take care, brother."

At the time, his breakout single "I Don't Want to Be" was gaining momentum. His album Chariot had just been released under J Records, and his career was about to take off. But what left the impression wasn't the fame; it was the posture. The willingness to help, to connect, to carry a bag as if it were second nature. That's not something you can train. That's who he was.

I've thought about that moment many times since, and I've shared this chance encounter with various people over the years, particularly when discussing leadership and brand values. The experience strengthened a belief I hold close: no matter how successful you become, your legacy still matters. In the end, people will stick with you because of who you are, not just what you offer. The real return on culture isn't just in retention or profits, it's in reputation. It's what people carry with them after the job is done and the elevator doors close.

The Secret Weapon: Culture Isn't Just Nice—It's Profitable

We often overestimate the impact of grand gestures and underestimate the influence of steady consistency. As previously discussed, culture is built in hallway conversations, the way performance is evaluated, the method in which we deliver bad news, and how feedback is received. It shows up in whether credit is shared or hoarded, and whether mistakes are treated as coaching moments or turned into ammunition. Everyday interactions may not feel seismic at the time and may seem small, almost forgettable, but over time they add up. Those ordinary moments create the predictability that develops safety, confidence, and momentum. They layer loyalty, pride, and resilience in a way that bonuses, branding, or mission statements can't replicate.

Time and again, we see that workplace performance management often fails to deliver results. There must be something bigger that drives employees and motivates them to achieve greatness. If you want a world-class culture, you must foster world-class leadership everywhere, not just at the top. Multiple studies confirm it. A Deloitte study found that companies with positive workplace cultures experience 30 percent higher levels of innovation and further outperform their competitors by as much as 200 percent in financial metrics over time (Abundance Global, 2024).[23]

Let's dig into some numbers.

Deloitte's 'Global Human Capital Trends' aims to find the balance in this complex world between productivity, expectations,

---

[23] Abundance Global. The ROI of company culture: Why investing in teams pays. Abundance Global, August 20, 2024. https://www.abundance.global/roi-company-culture-teams-pays/

and culture.[24] The implications are clear: strong cultures consistently outperform weak ones. One study shows that organizations that prioritize and invest in a strong workplace culture consistently outperform their peers across key business metrics. Positive cultures report 30 percent higher innovation and 40 percent better employee retention. High-performing cultures also experience 59 percent less turnover, which results in savings of 90 percent to 200 percent of an employee's annual salary per person retained.

And the financial implications extend even further. Organizations with strong cultural foundations enjoy 21 percent higher profitability and 17 percent improved productivity—cultures that foster psychological safety drive 27 percent more patents and 74 percent more leading-edge innovation. Simply put, when people feel safe, they take risks that move businesses forward. Engagement also pays off on the customer front, with connected employees delivering 10 percent higher satisfaction scores and generating 20 percent more in sales. These outcomes are not coincidental; they're the return on culture done right.

But if you want to know whether your investment in workplace culture is paying off, you need a basic plan to track progress. Here's how to do it in everyday terms:

1. **Start by knowing where you're at.**
   Look at key numbers such as employee turnover, absenteeism, productivity, job satisfaction, and the frequency of new ideas being shared. These are your starting points—or your "baseline."

2. **Try specific, meaningful changes.**
   Introduce targeted efforts to enhance the culture, such as employee recognition, wellness support, coaching,

---

[24] Deloitte. "Human Capital Trends." Deloitte Insights. https://www2.deloitte.com/us/en/insights/focus/human-capital-trends.html

or improved communication systems. Don't try to do everything at once; instead, focus on the efforts that align with your most significant gaps.

3. **Watch for both obvious and hidden results.**
Track direct improvements *(like fewer people quitting or lower costs)* and less visible wins *(like better morale, new ideas, or a stronger reputation)*. These indirect effects often pay off big over time.

4. **Do the math.**
To measure return on investment (ROI), use a simple formula:
ROI = (What You Gained - What You Spent) ÷ What You Spent × 100
If you saved $100,000 and spent $25,000 to achieve this, your ROI (Return on Investment) is 75 percent. That tells you it was a worthwhile investment.

<u>**What Does That Mean?**</u>
You earned three times what you spent.
For every $1 invested, you gained $3 back. That's a 300 percent return, which clearly signals that your investment in culture paid off in real financial terms.

Measuring What Matters

Measuring the return on culture is both an art and a discipline. Many leaders stumble not because they lack good intent but because they skip the fundamentals. The biggest mistake is failing to establish a baseline, without clear starting data, progress becomes invisible. Another is chasing instant results; culture change moves at the speed of trust, not the speed of quarterly reports. And perhaps the most overlooked? The hidden costs of leadership time, communication, and coordination. Companies need to understand that cultural work isn't free; it's an investment.

The good news is that data now proves what intuition has long suggested: culture isn't a soft concept; it's a hard advantage. Deloitte's *Global Human Capital Trends* reports that companies investing intentionally in culture outperform peers by up to 200 percent in key metrics like innovation, retention, and profitability. Take these two examples:

Case Study #1
One financial services firm invested $1.2 million in a cultural transformation and earned nearly $7.8 million in returns—a 548 percent ROI.[25] Here is the impact of their commitment:

- Employee turnover was reduced by 24 percent, saving about $3.4 million
- Productivity rose by 16 percent, adding an estimated $2.1 million in value
- Absenteeism decreased by 31 percent, saving an additional $780,000
- Customer satisfaction increased by 22 percent, resulting in $1.5 million more in revenue

Case Study #2
Culture-related investments can produce measurable results even in highly process-driven industries like manufacturing. One manufacturing company invested $850,000 in targeted safety and employee engagement initiatives, achieving significant operational and financial gains.

- The organization experienced a 41 percent decrease in safety incidents, resulting in $2.3 million in savings. Additionally, there was an 18 percent reduction in production errors, resulting in $1.1 million in additional savings.

[25] Enculture.ai. Culture by the numbers: The ROI of workplace culture investments. https://www.enculture.ai/blog/culture-by-the-numbers-the-roi-of-workplace-culture-investments

- Turnover among technicians declined by 26 percent, leading to $1.9 million in cost avoidance related to hiring, training, and lost productivity.

Overall, the investment generated a return of $5.3 million—equivalent to a 524 percent ROI. These examples clearly show that culture is not a cost center; it's a driver of performance. When organizations treat culture as a business system, the results show up everywhere: higher productivity, lower turnover, fewer errors, and stronger customer loyalty. The return isn't just emotional, it's operational and financial.

These aren't anomalies; they're evidence that culture drives profitability. I witnessed this firsthand at Dutch Bros. When I joined, the average tenure of leadership was over fifteen years, an almost unheard-of occurrence in the service industry. That stability wasn't luck; it was a matter of culture. Double-digit AUV growth, record customer satisfaction, and effortless market expansion all stemmed from one thing: trust built through values with culture as the multiplier.

Research confirms this. Oxford's Saïd Business School found that happy, engaged employees are 13 percent more productive.[26] A related study by Bellet, De Neve, and Ward (2020) proved a direct causal link between happiness and output. Every one-point increase in happiness drove roughly a 12 percent productivity gain.[27]

An additional landmark study by Gallup found that companies with highly engaged employees outperform their competitors

---

[26] University of Oxford. "Happy Workers Are 13% More Productive, Study Finds." University of Oxford News, October 24, 2019. https://www.ox.ac.uk/news/2019-10-24-happy-workers-are-13-more-productive

[27] Bellet, C. S., De Neve, J.E., & Ward, G. Does employee happiness have an impact on productivity? Management Science, 70(3), 1656–1679. 2023. https://doi.org/10.1287/mnsc.2023.4766

by 147 percent in earnings per share (EPS).[28] This isn't just a small increase; it's a clear sign that employee engagement is not a soft, feel-good metric but a significant factor driving financial results. EPS is a key indicator of how much profit a company generates for each outstanding share of stock, and it's closely monitored by investors and leaders. When engagement is high, employees tend to be more productive, loyal, and likely to provide better customer service, all of which support sustained business growth. Teams that feel connected to their work typically innovate more, communicate more effectively, and stay committed through changes and challenges. In short, investing in company culture isn't just about retention or morale; it's about creating a workforce that strengthens the entire business, making it more resilient and profitable.

In other words, culture isn't a "soft" metric; it's one of the clearest drivers of financial returns.

That's the power of culture-driven ROI; it's visible on the balance sheet, but its real influence runs even deeper. Numbers can capture growth, productivity, and customer loyalty, but they only tell part of the story. Culture works in ways that traditional financial models often struggle to quantify. It strengthens conviction and creates a foundation where leadership and collaboration naturally thrive. And that's where organizations need to broaden their lens, looking beyond immediate returns to understand the long-term, strategic value culture delivers.

If culture can directly influence your company's market performance and investor confidence, can you really afford to dismiss it as an option? If you're a leader who still thinks "culture stuff" sounds fluffy, think again.

---

[28] Kehoe, Julie. "Employee Engagement Delivers Positive Returns." Gallup, 2 May 2013.

The ROI of Joy: Why Happiness Pays Off

"Take care of your employees and they'll take care of your business."

–Richard Branson

For years, leaders have assumed that tighter systems and sharper tools drive results. However, research reveals something far more powerful and simpler: happy employees consistently outperform their peers.

A landmark study in *Management Science* (*Does Employee Happiness Have an Impact on Productivity*) by Bellet, De Neve, and Ward (2019) tracked nearly 1,800 British Telecom call-center employees over six months and uncovered a clear causal link between happiness and productivity. **Most notably,** the researchers found a clever, quasi-experimental way to isolate happiness from other variables by analyzing workers' exposure to weather. Call centers with more windows provided workers with a better view of the bright or gloomy skies, which in turn affected their mood.

Here's what they found:

- A one-point increase in happiness (on a 10-point scale) resulted in 12 percent more sales per week, equivalent to over three additional sales for workers whose weekly average was approximately twenty-five.

- Happier employees weren't necessarily working longer hours. They were simply more effective at their jobs: converting more calls into sales and navigating complex conversations with ease.

- The productivity boost was most pronounced in more emotionally demanding tasks, like re-contracting and selling bundled services. This highlights the power of positive affect in customer interactions.

- Workers in happier moods adhered more closely to their workflow schedules, took fewer breaks, and worked slightly faster. But the largest impact wasn't just effort; it was cognitive clarity and emotional agility.

The researchers estimate that even a modest lift–a one-standard-deviation increase in happiness–can result in a 30 percent increase in weekly sales. That's not a hypothetical; it's a statistically significant, field-tested return on emotional investment. And the business implications are massive. When 87 percent of executives agree that workplace happiness gives them a competitive advantage, yet fewer than 20 percent have an intentional strategy to improve it, it's clear we're sitting on untapped ROI. Happiness is the infrastructure for performance.

The same pattern appears across industries. Oxford's Saïd Business School found that engaged employees are 13 percent more productive than their disengaged peers. Taken together, these findings make one thing clear: happiness drives output as reliably as any operational metric.

However, culture isn't only validated by financial markets; it's also studied in depth in academia. Scholars like Dr. Yemisi Bolade-Ogunfodun remind us that behind the numbers lies something more nuanced: culture as lived experience, where values transform into behaviors and shared meaning. Her research reframes culture as the daily patterns of identity, interaction, and decision-making that shape real organizations. In other words, it's how values show up in practice, how people speak, decide, and work together. She challenges organizations to move beyond superficial value statements and instead embed cultural values into everyday actions. Culture exists in the spaces between individuals, where beliefs are lived out rather than merely listed.[29]

---

[29] Bolade-Ogunfodun, Y., Sinnicks, M., Akrivou, K., & Scalzo, G. "Exploring the Vulnerability of Practice-like Activities: an Ethnographic

Culture, at its core, sets the rhythm for everything that follows: how fast teams adapt, how deeply they collaborate, and how much ownership they bring to the table. It's the force that turns strategy into execution and plans into performance. Companies that neglect it often find themselves spending heavily on recruitment, marketing, and recovery from preventable failures, while those that invest in it enjoy momentum that money can't buy.

Since 1998, companies on the Fortune 100 Best Companies to Work For list have outperformed the market by approximately 3 times to 3.5 times. For example, Great Place to Work's '100 Best Index' shows 1,709 percent cumulative returns versus 526 percent for the Russell 3000 (through 2020), with similar outperformance persisting through 2024.[30]

If you're chasing bottom-line growth, don't just tweak processes, build joy. Culture compounds like interest; small, daily deposits that can multiply into exponential returns. Think about dropping a pebble into a pond: the ripple doesn't stay small. It grows outward, touching more water than you could ever trace back to that first tiny drop. Culture works in a similar way, where small actions, such as a simple "thank you," recognition, or a leader showing up unexpectantly, spread farther than you can measure, shaping performance, loyalty, and the organization's future. Small acts of attention that build trust, energy, and long-term resilience. Over time, these moments become the foundation of performance.

Positive culture costs almost nothing to create—yet its return is extraordinary. In an increasingly competitive world, the most

Perspective." Frontiers in Sociology, 7, Article 1003741. 2022. https://doi.org/10.3389/fsoc.2022.1003741

[30] Yoshimoto, C., & Erb, M. Treating employees well led to higher stock prices during the pandemic. Great Place To Work, August 5, 2021. https://www.greatplacetowork.com/resources/blog/treating-employees-well-led-to-higher-stock-prices-during-the-pandemic

sustainable differentiator isn't price, product, or process; it's people. And when people feel seen, supported, and inspired, they deliver results that no algorithm or efficiency tool can replicate.

In other words, joy isn't a soft priority; it's a hard, measurable advantage. Build it, nurture it, and your culture will repay you in ways the balance sheet can't fully capture, but your customers, employees, and community will absolutely feel.

"The way to develop the best that is in a person is by appreciation and encouragement." –Charles Schwab

How This Connects to a No EGO Mindset

This is the moment to ask yourself: Is your culture a competitive advantage, or your blind spot?

- **Culture drives performance.** Companies with strong cultures can experience revenue growth rates up to four times higher than those without.

- **Values are strategic.** When embedded authentically, they influence every interaction and decision.

- **Culture must be co-created.** It's not dictated from the top down; it's shaped by everyone, every day.

- **Inclusion pays off.** Diverse executive teams outperform their peers, and companies that prioritize equity and belonging encourage greater problem-solving and engagement.

- **Employee support equals customer success.** When your people thrive, they serve your customers better because they're aligned, empowered, and committed.

Protecting your culture is protecting the future. Guard it with intention. When leaders nurture love, consistency, and courage, they weave those values into the very DNA of their organization. That's how culture endures, built as a living force that inspires every choice.

When culture is strong, people rise. And when they do, everything rises with them.

Choose wisely! The culture you build today becomes the legacy others inherit tomorrow.

CHAPTER 8

Cultural Warriors

"When the storm hits, it's not your product that saves you—it's your people. And what holds them together is culture."

A Radical Way to Hire

At Dutch Bros, recruitment isn't just a transaction, but a celebration of people and possibility. Before the pandemic, shops didn't host interviews; they threw "hiring parties." Picture it: loud music blasting across the lot, string lights swaying in the evening breeze, baristas dancing in a ballroom, and company leaders cheering from the sidelines. It didn't feel like a job fair. It felt like a block party.

In that atmosphere, you didn't need polished answers; you just needed presence and heart. And you could spot it instantly. The ones who walked in with bold smiles, greeted strangers like old friends, and weren't afraid to clap to the beat of the music were the ones who lit up the room. The hiring team wasn't looking for experience as much as energy, seeking people who made others feel alive and who could capitalize on joy.

Sometimes the most memorable moments came from people who arrived shy or unsure, only to loosen up in the energy of the night. Maybe they started off quietly, but before long, they were laughing with strangers, high-fiving their peers, or even sparking a spontaneous dance line that had the whole group smiling. It wasn't about coffee knowledge or résumés but bringing light to the room.

In those moments, it became obvious who would be in line for an interview. The people who lifted the mood of everyone around them weren't just applying for a job; they were already shaping the culture. Those were the future cultural warriors of the brand. People who are not chasing a paycheck, but rather a connection. In the long run they would turn into employees who wanted to make every day joyful, would carry that spark to encourage their teammates, or brighten the mood of a groggy customer at 5 a.m.

That's where the real magic would begin. Dutch Bros believed that culture was created in small, ordinary moments: shared laughs over spilled coffee, dancing inside the shops, wearing colorful outfits, or more consequential acts, such as a teammate picking up an extra shift without being asked, or a quiet word of encouragement before the morning rush. Those sparks, when multiplied daily, become the proof of the "inverse pyramid" in action. When culture is alive at the front lines, leadership feels it all the way to the top.

That joy is the oxygen of Dutch Bros. It powers customer smiles, team resilience, and brand loyalty. It is a strategy disguised as spirit, and it proved that the right people weren't just employees. They were the culture.

The True Guardians of Culture: Hiring and Empowering the Right People

When leaders invest in teams through recognition, joy, and interaction, employees respond by providing better service. That service builds loyal customers, and those loyal customers, in turn, increase revenue, drive growth, and contribute to the long-term success of the business.

Every employee, to some extent, is a culture warrior. Whether that influence strengthens or erodes what's been built depends entirely on what they model and reinforce in others. One of the most significant shifts a leader can inspire is reframing leadership as service, not authority, ensuring it is quiet, situational, and rooted in accountability. True leadership begins with the mindset that says, *"I take responsibility for the experience I create for others."*

When enough people adopt that approach, culture becomes self-sustaining. But that doesn't happen by accident; it happens through the people you bring into the fold. Most companies can teach technical skills, processes, and policies, but what you cannot teach is heart, humility, grit, or a genuine desire to serve. That's why hiring isn't just about experience; it's about character and energy.

When building a business where love and leadership matter, you must guard the gates, not to keep people out, but to ensure you're inviting the right ones in. Culture is inclusive by design but selective by necessity.

At Dutch Bros, we used to say, "Protect the vibe," because one wrong hire—someone negative, selfish, or passive-aggressive—can do more damage to the culture than missing a sales target.

Hiring for cultural fit is a discipline that demands intentionality at every stage, from the job descriptions you craft to the way you interview and onboard new hires. When done effectively, hiring shifts from being just an HR task to becoming a leadership art form that sculpts culture one decision at a time.

The starting point is clarity. Define your non-negotiables: the traits your culture absolutely needs to thrive, like humility, positivity, adaptability, ownership, or kindness. Until you name them, you risk hiring qualified strangers who may never truly feel at home. Until you define what "right" looks like, you risk hiring well-qualified strangers who may never truly belong.

When you sit across from a candidate, look beyond the résumé. Ask about the challenging moments. How did they respond to failure? How do they speak about former teammates or bosses? Do they use "we" or "I"? Tone often tells the truth faster than content. If you sense arrogance, blame, or entitlement, then pause. Sometimes the right person needs a better question to reveal their heart. But if those red flags persist, believe what you see. You're not just filling a role; you're inviting someone into your story.

Skills can be developed; character is much harder to alter. Once you find someone who fits in, embrace them as family. Culture isn't just about guarding the gates; it's about opening your arms wide when someone truly belongs.

The Artform of Hiring: Protecting the Vibe in the Shops

Hiring is choreography. At Dutch Bros, it looked more like a block party than a boardroom. Here's how that energy became a system, structured joy with purpose:

Stage	What It Looks Like in Action	Why It Matters to Culture
The Invitation	Instead of a stiff job posting, create an experience that feels like an open door—music, lights, laughter. People don't "apply"; they're invited to join something bigger.	The tone is set from the first moment. Applicants feel energy, not bureaucracy.
The First Impression	No résumés first. Watch how someone walks into the room, how they greet a stranger, how their smile changes the space.	You hire for presence, not paper. If they can lift a room in thirty seconds, they'll encourage a team for years.
The Test of Joy	In a hiring party, you see how candidates interact with baristas, customers, and each other. Do they clap, laugh, join in, or sit back?	Culture is contagious. You're looking for carriers of joy.
The Conversation	Ask about the last time they helped someone, not the last software they used. Stories of kindness, grit, or fun are stronger predictors than technical bullet points.	People reveal values in stories. It's harder to fake a heart than credentials.

Stage	What It Looks Like in Action	Why It Matters to Culture
The Decision	Instead of a panel interview, the team decides together: Did this person protect the vibe? Did they amplify it? Would you want to spend a tough shift with them?	Culture is collective. If the crew feels the spark, it's a safe bet the customers will too.
The Welcome	Once chosen, the new hire is celebrated and cheered on—with high-fives, music, and maybe even confetti. Joining isn't small; it's a moment.	When you make hiring a celebration, people know they didn't just get a job, they joined a movement.

"Hire character. Train skill."
—Peter Schutz (former Porsche CEO)

The Trader Joe's Way: The Power of Who You Hire

In the book "Becoming Trader Joe," Joe Coulombe clearly states that the brand's success began with hiring the right people.[31]

He didn't necessarily seek applicants with retail experience, but valued those who were friendly, curious, and aligned with the brand's values. Trader Joe's hiring process focused on personality rather than pedigree. Interviews were often conducted in multiple rounds with store leaders, such as "mates" and "captains," who looked for attitude, warmth, and the ability to connect with others.

Even today, Trader Joe's rarely advertises store roles, as customers, family, friends of employees, or others who hear about

---

[31] Coulombe, Joe. "Becoming Trader Joe: How I Did Business My Way and Still Beat the Big Guys." HarperCollins Leadership, 2021.

Trader Joe's are often drawn to the business through reputation and referral. Formal experience isn't required; fit is. What matters most is whether you can connect, care, and contribute to the store's unique atmosphere.

Coulombe also recognized that providing excellent customer service begins with taking care of your people. Trader Joe's offers above-average pay, full benefits and premiums for weekends. The culture is intentionally lively and collaborative. Hawaiian shirts, hand-drawn chalkboard signs, and open dialogue aren't just gimmicks; they are part of a workplace where everyone is encouraged to have fun and encouraged to wear joy as their uniform. Employees become brand ambassadors because they feel like owners.

However, Trader Joe's isn't alone. In-N-Out Burger built its reputation on the same foundation. Since its founding in 1948 by Harry and Esther Snyder, the company has emphasized hiring for attitude and authenticity over experience. As Lynsi Snyder recounts in *The Ins-N-Outs of In-N-Out Burger*, she began her career at seventeen as an hourly associate, rotating through various roles to gain a comprehensive understanding of the business.[32] That path isn't unusual, as about 80 percent of managers started as crew members, advancing through demonstrated fit, competence, and cultural alignment.

SmartBrief notes that this values-based approach to hiring reinforces traits like integrity, honesty, and respect through recruiting and onboarding, ensuring that the culture is lived from day one.[33]

---

[32] Snyder, Lynsi. The Ins-N-Outs of In-N-Out Burger: The Inside Story of California's First Drive-Through and How it Became a Beloved Cultural Icon. Thomas Nelson, 2023.

[33] SmartBrief Editors. "How In-N-Out Burger Maintains Its Strong Culture as It Grows." SmartBrief, 4 May 2022. https://corp.smartbrief.com/original/2022/05/how-in-n-out-burger-maintains-its-strong-culture-as-it-grows

And the results show. In-N-Out's average manager earns over $120,000 per year, turnover is a fraction of industry norms and tenure averages fourteen years. In a world obsessed with growth, they've scaled loyalty.

Empowerment: Letting Your People Take Ownership

Hiring the right people is only the start; culture lives through how people are empowered. This empowerment begins with setting clear expectations and shared goals, and grows when people are trusted with meaningful work. The leader's job is not to dictate, but to coach, stay curious, provide feedback, and remain committed to each person's growth.

These ideas aren't abstract; they became essential when we started developing the Construction Department at Dutch Bros to meet the company's aggressive growth targets. The pressure created unease across the team. Construction Managers felt nervous about meeting deadlines, Directors worried about their own commitments, and support teams—Design, Equipment, and Project Coordinators—doubted whether the schedules were even achievable. Instead of grabbing the reins out of fear, we collaborated to create an execution plan. It wasn't about dictating outcomes; it was about fostering a growth mindset that enabled the team to work through schedules, manage consultants, and address challenges as they arose. While I helped facilitate the process, the real support and encouragement came from leaders across the team and throughout the departments we served.

Things went wrong, of course—but mistakes became lessons, not liabilities. Postmortems focused on "What would you do differently next time?" rather than "Who's to blame?" That mindset shift turned fear into focus. Over time, consistency and coaching replaced chaos and correction. The team not only met expectations, but they also became leaders who carried the culture forward.

Real empowerment happens when growth is built into the culture. The goal isn't perfection; it's progress. When people understand both their responsibilities and the "why" behind them, they act with ownership and pride–that's how leadership multiplies.

> *"The best companies don't just have a mission statement–they have missionaries."*
> –John Doerr

The Loyalty Loop: Why Culture Scales from Within

In her article "Customer Loyalty Starts with Employee Engagement," Alison Zook builds on a powerful insight from Simon Sinek: "Customers will never love a company until the employees love it first."[34] She makes a compelling case that employee engagement isn't just an HR initiative, but a critical business imperative. When employees feel genuinely valued, supported, and connected to their work, that sense of purpose becomes contagious. It fuels more authentic and energized interactions, creating a ripple effect that customers can feel.

As Zook illustrates, a culture rooted in care and commitment internally will almost always translate to consistency and excellence externally. Just as disengaged employees can damage brand reputation through indifference, engaged employees act as brand ambassadors. Whether on the sales floor or behind the scenes, their belief in the brand influences how they present themselves. That belief becomes a lived experience, one that customers can feel. In this way, employee engagement isn't a soft metric; it's a human driver of customer loyalty and long-term business success. Research shows that companies

---

[34] Zook, Alison. "Customer Loyalty Starts with Employee Engagement." Arcade.co, July 7, 2020. https://www.arcade.co/post/customer-loyalty-starts-with-employee-engagement

with highly engaged employees outperform their competition by 148 percent in earnings per share. One example of this principle in action is In-N-Out Burger, which has embedded disciplined hiring and leadership development into its DNA.

The dedication to finding and developing the right people is best demonstrated by In-N-Out University, founded by Rich Snyder in 1977 and established as a formal training center by 1984 on the Baldwin Park property. Entry-level associates advance through eight clearly defined development stages, from backroom and counter service to cook and supervisor, ensuring that every manager has mastered each operational role before leading teams. Managers then attend In-N-Out University to deepen their understanding of the brand's values and operational standards, participating in in-person sessions and engaging directly in new store openings. This tightly controlled, family-run training system supports In-N-Out's deliberate growth and maintains its culture of quality, freshness, and hospitality at every location. Leadership advancement is grounded in values-driven principles, consistency, and cultural alignment, ensuring the company's core ethos remains strong as it grows.

By contrast, *McDonald's Hamburger University* (HU) was first launched in 1961.[35] During my tenure at McDonald's, I had the opportunity to witness firsthand the scale of Hamburger University, located in Oak Brook, IL, as I attended it several times. Today, with satellite campuses worldwide, HU operates on a more global, franchise-focused scale. It trains over 5,000 employees annually, including managers and franchisees, through formal programs that cover operations, leadership,

---

[35] McDonald's Corporation. "Hamburger University: Developing Leaders Around the World." McDonalds.com.
https://corporate.mcdonalds.com/corpmcd/our-people/training-and-education/hamburger-university.html

and customer experience, and even offers college credit toward business degrees.

While both universities are designed to build leaders who embody their brand's culture, In-N-Out's model emphasizes depth and cultural consistency, training managers only from within the company and in small cohorts. In contrast, McDonald's emphasizes breadth, standardization, and scale across diverse global markets.

Ultimately, the comparison reveals two equally effective, yet distinct, approaches to leadership development: one driven by cultural preservation and controlled growth, and the other, designed for global consistency and franchise scalability. Each reflects the values the company chooses to guard most fiercely: freshness and family at In-N-Out, as well as standardization and systemic repeatability at McDonald's.

The Hand That Carries the Culture

It is essential to realize that culture is not static. It grows stronger or weaker with every person you bring into your business, every behavior you tolerate, and every action you celebrate. Each new hire is either a builder or a breaker. When you look at a job candidate, don't just ask, "Can they do the job?" Ask, "Will they strengthen and protect the culture?"

The HR department can assist with systems and background checks, but leadership is responsible for the culture. They hold the key and influence the ripple effects. You're not just filling seats; it's about filling the room with the kind of people who lift others higher. Each hiring decision becomes a leadership choice, and every interview is an opportunity to invest in legacy.

No matter how advanced your strategies, how innovative your products, or how bold your growth plans, your organization's core will always be your people. Behind every number, every customer review, and every innovation is a human being who has chosen to contribute their talents and energy to your mission. When people believe in what they're building, they don't just contribute to culture, they *carry* it. They become storytellers of your values, translating belief into action, and turning everyday moments into expressions of identity.

That's why building and protecting culture isn't a side task; it's the core of sustainable success. Hiring someone who genuinely believes in your mission doesn't just fill a role; it multiplies momentum. You're inviting a builder of dreams, protectors of the vibe, and future storytellers who will carry your values far beyond what you can predict.

There is real science that backs it up. The *Cambridge Handbook of Workplace Affect* shows that employees' moods, especially smiles, are contagious. A genuine smile from an employee can boost a customer's mood and shape their entire experience.[36] Customers often unconsciously mirror these expressions, which can elevate their mood, strengthen satisfaction, and foster loyalty. In service industries, this silent emotional exchange significantly enhances perceived service quality and increases the likelihood of customers returning with a positive experience. It's subtle, but powerful and the kind of thing that can only happen when an employee is genuinely engaged.

That's the invisible power of culture; it's contagious. The best leaders understand that it spreads through example.

> *"When people go to work, they shouldn't have to leave their hearts at home."*
> —Betty Bender

---

[36] Russell, James A., and Lisa Feldman Barrett, eds. "The Cambridge Handbook of Workplace Affect". Cambridge University Press, 2021. https://www.cambridge.org/core/books/cambridge-handbook-of-workplace-affect/EBFED416C157F1ECCD0CEE3ED69DCE5B

From Tasks to Meaning

Culture and collaboration go beyond office design; they're fostered through intentional and engaging systems. Arcade is one example, showing how training and recognition can become a game people actually want to play. Instead of static videos or endless quizzes, employees sharpen real-world skills through AI-powered coaching that simulates customer interactions and provides instant, measurable feedback. Learning feels less like school and more like practice with a purpose.

That energy carries into everyday performance. Leaderboards update live, contests spark bursts of excitement, and micro-incentives keep the momentum going with small but meaningful rewards. Recognition is woven directly into the flow of work—peers can celebrate each other with digital badges and shout-outs, making success visible in real time. The effect is contagious: instead of waiting for annual reviews, employees see their progress daily, and the team shares in those wins together.

One Arcade user put it simply: "Our best sellers teach their peers; this has proven more impactful than asking them to watch videos or complete quizzes—it makes our company culture stronger and keeps a big organization feeling small." That's the cultural multiplier—performance becomes collaborative, not competitive, and culture grows stronger.

Research reinforces these outcomes. A Korn Ferry study found that engaged workers are 43 percent more productive than their disengaged peers. That added capacity creates what researchers call time capital—the ability to reinvest energy into customers and teammates without additional head count. Similarly, Greg Oldham and Richard Hackman's Work Redesign highlights the concept of "task significance": When employees see how their work improves others' lives, they shift from merely completing tasks to creating meaningful impact. That shift is the cultural spark that fuels loyalty on both sides of the counter.

Zappos: The Gold Standard in Service-Driven Culture

Take Zappos. Known for its legendary customer service, it famously allows reps to stay on the phone as long as needed, with one historic call lasting more than ten hours. They've even delivered shoes from competitor stores just to help a customer in need. But the magic behind those stories isn't a quirky policy; it's culture. Founder Tony Hsieh recognized that only engaged and empowered employees would go the extra mile to serve others.

When he reimagined Zappos' headquarters, Hsieh wasn't just aiming for an open floor plan. He was designing a space to foster connections among people. The building's layout directed employees through shared areas to encourage what he called "collision-able hours." Whether at a coffee bar, a lounge, or during playful events like "Bald & Blue Day," these encounters sparked spontaneous moments of connection that boosted collaboration and reinforced a shared identity.

Hsieh also extended this philosophy beyond his company. Through the Downtown Project in Las Vegas, he expanded the experiment to the community by funding coworking hubs, speaker series, and collaborative workspaces. His goal was the same: to make chance encounters intentional and to increase creativity both within the company and across the city.

Why does this matter? Because culture doesn't appear on its own, it's shaped by the spaces people occupy, the systems that guide them, and the relationships that hold them together. Zappos understood this well, creating an environment where connection, creativity, and loyalty were daily realities.

The deeper lesson is clear: the people you bring in and the way you lead them ultimately define the story your culture tells. Hiring, development, and leadership are cultural investments that reveal, with clarity, the future you are building.

CHAPTER 9

Cultivating a Culture of Development

"Before you are a leader, success is all about growing yourself. When you become a leader, success is all about growing others."

–Jack Welch

Dutch Bros Story from a Loyal Customer

"I want to take a moment to recognize an extraordinary young man named Josh at your Surprise, AZ location.

My mom had stopped by to order drinks for our family when she noticed a few employees dancing playfully near the window. With a smile and a bit of boldness, she jokingly asked for her drink… "with a dance." Without missing a beat, Josh asked, "Do you two-step?" Surprised and delighted, she said, "Yes."

He smiled, walked out to her car, turned on George Strait, and gently took her hand for a dance in the parking lot.

What Josh didn't know was that this small moment carried the weight of something much bigger. A year ago this month, my mom lost her husband unexpectedly. The last song they danced to was George Strait.

For Josh, it may have been just a fun moment of kindness. But for my mom, it was the first time she had danced since losing the love of her life. In that simple, thoughtful act, he gave her something incredibly meaningful: a moment of joy, remembrance, and healing.

I can't thank your team enough for the spirit they bring to work every day. Josh went above and beyond in a way that touched our entire family. And Jeremy, thank you for your kindness and care.

You've earned a lifelong customer not just through service, but through sincere humanity."

What Josh did that day wasn't just kind, it was cultural. That freedom to care is what creates lasting loyalty, both in customers and in communities. It's a living example of the No EGO mindset in action. He turned an ordinary moment into something extraordinary by living the company's values.

That's where culture becomes leadership in its purest form, when it's written on your employees' hearts. This ripple effect of leadership is the quiet influence that spreads when one person chooses to act with love, courage, and authenticity. And when that happens across a team, it doesn't just change moments; it changes everything.

The Leadership Imperative: Be a Ripple Starter

There's a famous saying: "The standard you walk past is the standard you accept." This was said during a speech by Lieutenant General David Morrison, former Chief of the Australian Army. The phrase has since become a rallying call in leadership and culture-building discussions, emphasizing the importance of accountability and modeling the behaviors you expect.

If you see someone treating a colleague disrespectfully and say nothing, you are saying it's acceptable. If you hear gossip and join in, even if only silently, you are contributing to a negative culture. If you know something could be better but don't speak up because "it's not my place," you're reinforcing the status quo.

Culture is shaped not just by what we celebrate, but by what we tolerate.

Leadership is not simply about hitting KPIs or closing deals. It's about starting ripples, those small actions that may seem ordinary at the moment, but over time accumulate into the heartbeat of the organization. A leader who shows up with optimism on a tough project day can revitalize the energy of the entire room. They can handle setbacks with grace instead of blame and teach resilience through their example. Sometimes it's simply a teammate who brings empathy during moments of conflict, quietly raising the bar for everyone around them.

Every day, whether we realize it or not, we create ripples through our actions. Every "thank you" spoken with sincerity, every honest check-in, and every moment of genuine recognition are not just side notes to the mission; they are the mission. The culture we discuss in meetings or strategies only comes alive when people see it in action. It's not taught once; it's modeled daily. It is caught in how people experience leadership and in the ways they see behavior modeled consistently. This is the mission!

As leaders, we must ask ourselves: How am I showing up? Who am I lifting today? How am I reinforcing the kind of culture I want to see grow? Leadership is a living force. One leader planting seeds of trust can grow an entire forest of loyalty. Another leader modeling humility can create a pipeline of servant leaders who will carry that spirit forward long after the original leader has moved on. Another choice to walk the halls instead of hiding behind closed doors can transform a culture of silence into one of vibrant, open communication.

The impact of leadership is seldom immediate, but over time, it becomes undeniable. Never underestimate the power of your influence, for better or worse. You are never just an employee, a manager, or a teammate; you are an architect of the experiences others will remember. Every decision you make creates ripples outward.

Culture is revealed in daily behaviors, especially when values are put to the test. People take their cues from how leaders respond under pressure. If you show clarity, resilience, and consistency, your team will echo it. If you waver, they'll notice that too. In the end, it isn't language that earns loyalty, but the example you set when it matters most.

Building a Culture That Outlives You

If you want a culture that lasts, you can't just hire great people; you have to nurture them, water them, challenge them, stretch them, and sometimes even replant them when they outgrow their first role. A culture that doesn't invest in people will eventually crumble through missed opportunities, untapped potential, and fading dreams.

Trader Joe's is a company known for its deep commitment to internal promotion. Every full-time employee is cross-trained in multiple roles, including cashier, stocking, and store bookkeeping. This approach builds ownership, broadens understanding, and cultivates confidence. Coulombe believed that when you empower people with knowledge and give them responsibility, they rise to the challenge.

Leadership development wasn't built on formal programs; it grew from familiarity and shared experience. Most store managers (known as "captains") began their careers on the sales floor. When it was time to advance, candidates were assessed on technical skills, emotional intelligence, communication, and their ability to support those around them. Trader Joe's didn't outsource its culture; it raised its own leaders from within. Leaders were shaped by the same values they would eventually be responsible for upholding.

In the early days of Dutch Bros, there wasn't a deep bench of talent waiting outside the doors. Instead, they grew their own talent. The company identified talent early and invested in people, teaching leadership by living it out loud. They didn't wait for someone to be *ready;* they gave them a chance to rise, then cheered like crazy and supported them with enthusiasm until a Broista reached their full potential. Too many companies miss this opportunity; leaders aren't discovered, they're developed. When discussing the challenges of hiring the right *fit* for your brand and talent that elevates your business, looking outside isn't always the right option. You don't stumble across perfect managers like seashells on a beach. You build them, layer by layer, with mentorship, patience, and the courage to let them fall and rise again with the tides.

One of the greatest joys in leadership is having a front-row seat to someone else's glow-up. Honestly, there's nothing better than watching someone realize, "Wait. . .I'm actually good at this!" That moment when a person steps into their own greatness is pure gold. It's addictive. And it should be. But for people to shine, leaders must be intentional about giving them the light. That means creating opportunities, not waiting for them to appear, and recognizing potential in the ordinary moments most companies overlook.

> *"Leadership is unlocking people's potential to become better."*
>
> –Bill Bradley

Development Is Not an Event—It's a Lifestyle

Real development is a way of life woven into the daily rhythm of your business. It shows up in how you coach after a tough call, how you assign tasks before someone feels 100 percent ready, and how you celebrate their effort just as fiercely as their results.

At its core, development is built on two principles: belief and exposure. The belief that individuals can grow beyond their current limits, combined with exposure to experiences that push them outside their comfort zones, is key. Leadership can't be rushed; it grows through patient, consistent, intentional effort. Research supports this: the Center for Creative Leadership highlights that leadership development is not a one-time event, but an ongoing process integrated into daily work (Center for Creative Leadership, 2021).[37]

---

[37] Center for Creative Leadership. "Leadership Development Research: What Works and What Doesn't?" Center for Creative Leadership, April 22, 2021. https://www.ccl.org/articles/leading-effectively-articles/3-keys-making-leadership-development-work/.

1. Coaching Leadership
Research shows that when leaders mentor rather than control, employees experience higher psychological empowerment and creativity (Kim et al., 2023).[38] Coaching leaders doesn't involve stepping in to "fix" everything; instead, they are engaged, ask questions, and encourage people to think for themselves. Growth happens because people are trusted to stretch and discover.

2. Autonomy-Supportive Leadership
Similarly, environments that grant autonomy enhance engagement and intrinsic motivation, while controlling ones diminish them (Sarmah et al., 2021).[39] People thrive when they make their own decisions, face mistakes, and build confidence through experience.

3. Situational Leadership
Situational Leadership theory emphasizes that effective leaders adjust—sometimes guiding directly, sometimes stepping back—depending on what their people need at the moment (Hersey & Blanchard, 1969).[40] The instinct to know when to lead from the front and when to coach from the side is a skill that separates good leaders from great ones.

4. The Organizational Imperative
Organizations that embrace these principles don't wait for the perfect moment to develop talent. They start early, invest

[38] Kim, M., Han, J., Lee, J., and Choi, J. N. "Coaching Leadership and Employee creativity: the Mediating Roles of Psychological Empowerment and Voice Behavior." Frontiers in Psychology, 14, 1123456. 2023. https://doi.org/10.3389/fpsyg.2023.1008633
[39] Sarmah, R., Vanden Broeck, A., Leroy, H., and Vansteenkiste, M. "Autonomy-Supportive and Controlling Leadership: A Meta-Analysis of Their Relations with Employee Outcomes." Motivation and Emotion, 45(6), 789–812. 2021. https://doi.org/10.1007/s11031-021-09921-y
[40] Hersey, P., and Blanchard, K. H. "Life Cycle Theory of Leadership." Training and Development Journal, 23(5), 26–34. 1969.

steadily, and weave development into everyday work. Growth may be messy, but it remains an invaluable investment any culture can make in its people. In practice, this means knowing when to step in and when to hold back. The easy path is to fix problems for someone; the more complicated, but far more valuable, choice is to coach them toward their own solutions. People don't grow under constant supervision; they produce when they're trusted to make decisions, learn from mistakes, and recover.

Throughout my career, I have encouraged people to surprise me. I ask them to "Bring me three solutions, and then we'll talk." More often than not, their second or third idea will surpass my best ones. Giving someone the answer short-circuits their growth, but creating space for problem-solving nurtures their creativity and confidence and may even turn the leader into the student during the process.

At Dutch Bros, one of my favorite sayings was: "Coach the moment. Celebrate the effort. Build the future." Not every coaching moment calls for a formal sit-down. Some of the most meaningful growth occurs during casual conversations over coffee, hallway chats, or a simple "You got this" before a big meeting. Leadership isn't about perfection but about being present and willing to walk with others through the messy middle as they develop into their potential.

Not everyone's growth looks the same, and that's something to celebrate, even though it can be difficult to navigate. Some people aim to become managers, while others want to master their craft on the front lines. Still, others seek to develop entirely new solutions that have not been considered yet. If you only define success as "climbing the ladder," you'll overlook those who want to grow deeper, not just higher. That's why great cultures create multiple pathways for growth: leadership tracks for managers, specialist tracks for subject matter experts (SMEs), or modernization tracks for creative thinkers. Growth should feel personal, not robotic, and should be aligned with each person's talents, ambitions, and the unique role they are meant to fulfill. When you do this well, staying at your company doesn't mean staying stagnant; it means thriving, maturing, and growing into the professional you were meant to become.

One of the greatest gifts you can give someone is your belief in them, before they believe in themselves. Most people won't raise their hand for a bigger role until they feel "ready." But here's the truth: no one ever feels fully ready for their next level of growth. It's called *Imposter Syndrome*, and it's more common than we think. First coined in 1978 by psychologists Pauline Clance and Suzanne Imes, the term originally described high-achieving women who felt like frauds despite their success. Today, it's recognized as a widespread experience—especially among leaders—where capable individuals doubt their own abilities even while performing at high levels.[41]

A 2024 report, highlighted by Bloomberg, revealed that an astonishing 71 percent of U.S. CEOs admitted to experiencing imposter syndrome. This data reinforces what many executive coaches have long observed: the higher the position, the greater the pressure to appear confident, even when the path is unclear.[42]

---

[41] Clance, P. R., & Imes, S. A. "The Impostor Phenomenon in High Achieving Women: Dynamics and Therapeutic Intervention." Psychotherapy: Theory, Research & Practice, 15(3), 241–247. 1978.
[42] Bloomberg. "Imposter syndrome reported by 71% of CEOs." Bloomberg.com, June 25, 2024. https://www.bloomberg.com/news/newsletters/2024-06-25/imposter-syndrome-reported-by-71-of-ceos; Korn Ferry. "71% of U.S. CEOs experience symptoms of imposter syndrome [Press release]." June 6, 2024. https://www.kornferry.com/about-us/press/71percent-of-us-ceos-experience-imposter-syndrome-new-korn-ferry-research-finds

The article points out a stark reality: that many CEOs prepare diligently for 60 percent of the job, but the remaining 40 percent is navigated through instinct, improvisation, and resilience in real-time. Leadership, especially at the highest level, isn't about having all the answers, but about learning to move forward despite uncertainty, while inspiring confidence in others.

But the burden of uncertainty doesn't fall solely on the Executive Team. According to Korn Ferry's Workforce 2025 survey, 43 percent of workers say their leaders aren't aligned. Equally concerning, 43 percent of senior executives admit they're unsure if they can meet their responsibilities because of limited resources and increasing pressure.

This is a reminder that even the most senior leaders are still learners. That is why company boards are composed of experts from all disciplines, to help make decisions that are widely expected to enhance the business. Environments that foster vulnerability, reflection, and growth are not only healthier but also more sustainable. They're the kinds of cultures that endure.

This dual uncertainty, arising from both top-down and bottom-up perspectives, creates a void in the culture. When employees perceive a lack of clear leadership, productivity tends to decline—energy shifts from engagement to doubt. Clarity turns into confusion.

In addition to the rapid pace of change in today's business environment, the pressure to adopt emerging technologies like AI, robotics, and others, along with the constant call to innovate, it's no wonder many leaders feel overwhelmed. But this isn't a call for perfection; it's about alignment. Leaders need to openly acknowledge their limitations and create spaces for shared clarity. They must bring their teams into the conversation and involve them in solutions to strengthen resolve and activate purpose.

Strong cultures are built when leaders choose courage over comfort. The leaders who invite their people into the struggle, who are transparent in their uncertainty, and who are grounded in their values when pressure mounts, are the ones who leave behind a lasting legacy.

The Power of Credit: Real Leadership Lets Others Shine

Arguably, the most overlooked yet powerful tool in leadership is simple, free, and transformative: giving people credit. Recognition isn't just about compliments; it's about seeing others, elevating them, and creating a culture where contributions are noticed and celebrated. Research consistently shows that employees who feel recognized are more engaged, more productive, and significantly less likely to leave (Gallup, 2023).[43]

Great leaders go even further. They don't just share credit; they willingly give it away. They allow others to stand in the spotlight, even if the idea was influenced or guided by their leadership. They understand that ego and impact don't mix. Stepping back so others can move forward isn't a sign of weakness; it's a sign of wisdom. It's an investment in culture and confidence.

Patrick Lencioni reminds us that "the ultimate dysfunction of a team is the absence of trust" (The Five Dysfunctions of a Team, 2002).[44] Trust grows when people see that a power-hungry boss won't take credit for their efforts. In fact, leaders who openly recognize others' strengths, even those of subordinates, build credibility more quickly and promote a team that takes responsibility for its results.

---

[43] Gallup. "State of the Global Workplace Report". Gallup, 2023. https://www.gallup.com/workplace/349484/state-of-the-global-workplace.aspx
[44] Lencioni, Patrick. "The Five Dysfunctions of a Team: A Leadership Fable". Jossey-Bass. 2002.

Harvard Business Review agrees. In a 2020 article titled "Why Giving Credit Matters More Than You Think," researchers found that "leaders who regularly give credit to team members are viewed as more trustworthy, more competent, and more promotable."[45] They are also more respected. The reason is simple: people are drawn to leaders who elevate others, not those who hoard recognition.

Here's the paradox of leadership: the more you step back, the more you empower others, and it doesn't remove your influence; it amplifies it. A leader's legacy isn't built on how brightly they stand alone, but on how much light they help others carry. Your role as a leader is to create the conditions where confidence, performance, and growth flourish, because when they rise, you rise. In elevating them, you multiply the strength, resilience, and reach of the entire team. This ripple effect doesn't just strengthen one department; it signals across the whole organization what kind of culture is being built.

> *"The strength of the team is each individual member. The strength of each member is the team."*
> —Phil Jackson

Or said another way:

> *"For the strength of the Pack is the Wolf, and the strength of the Wolf is the Pack."*
> —Rudyard Kipling's *The Jungle Book*

The Stretch Zone: Where Leaders Are Made

Growth requires us to leave behind the comfort and security of what we already know and embrace the challenge of the

---

[45] Harvard Business Review. "Why Giving Credit Matters More Than You Think by David Burkus", 2020

unknown. This uncertainty and discomfort don't mean you're unqualified; it means you're expanding. Figuring it out as we go requires people to rely on past experiences, instinct, and the collective wisdom of their teams.

It's in that stretch zone, where the chaos, the pressure, and the unknown unleash the real transformation that happens. It's where leadership is forged and greatness grows. Ironically, it's often the very feeling of being uncomfortable or "unready" that proves you're precisely where you need to be.

Mentorship is about more than passing on knowledge—it's about believing in people before they believe in themselves. Great leaders don't wait for confidence to arrive; they create moments that build it. Sometimes it's giving someone a stretch project. Sometimes it's simply saying, "I believe you can handle this." And when those moments bring stumbles, leaders don't see failure—they see learning in motion, and they stand beside their people until confidence catches up with capability.

In my career, I've seen it repeatedly: the people who grow the fastest aren't the ones who feel the most confident at the start. They're the ones who were mentored and pushed beyond their comfort zone, then stand nearby, cheering and coaching when they needed it most. Stretch assignments aren't punishments; they're signals of belief. If you only ever give people what they're already good at, you'll never find out what else they're capable of. Growth lives at the edges. Push people kindly, wisely, and lovingly into their edges, and you'll be amazed at the leaders who emerge.

The Leaders You Choose Define the Culture You Keep

When it's time to promote someone, the instinct is to reward results. You look to the top producer, the deal closer, the one logging the longest hours or delivering the most significant wins. But performance alone doesn't guarantee leadership.

Some of the most gifted individual contributors are incredible drivers but thrive best in their own lanes. They may not be interested in leading others, but instead are chasing a title for recognition rather than readiness. Either way, promoting based solely on output risks overlooking the qualities that truly sustain culture.

The goal is to promote those who lift others, embody your values, and strengthen the team to build a culture of stewardship. Hustle may drive results, but heart sustains them. Research from Harvard Business Review, Gallup, and Deloitte shows that organizations promoting values-based leadership consistently see higher engagement, lower turnover, and stronger long-term performance.

Before promoting anyone, I ask three questions:

- Do they multiply energy or drain it?
- Do they build people up or quietly tear them down?
- Will they protect the culture, or put themselves above it?

When advancement reflects both results *and* values, it sends a powerful signal: this organization rewards not just what you achieve, but how you achieve it. People quickly learn whether leadership is a platform for ego or a commitment to the greater good.

In the end, leadership isn't a prize for achievement; it's a responsibility to serve.

Coaching with Both Hands: Challenge + Care

If you want to develop people, you must coach with both hands: one offering challenge, the other offering care. Too often, leaders rely too heavily on one side of the equation. Some only push harder, setting higher goals and tighter deadlines, driving performance at the expense of burnout. Others focus solely on encouragement, fostering goodwill, but failing to instill accountability or standards. Neither extreme fosters growth. Genuine leadership requires a balance: the courage to push people beyond their comfort zones and the empathy to support them as they learn. Challenge without care breeds resentment or fear; care without challenge leads to complacency. However, when leaders strike a balance between these two, they create the conditions for people to reach their full potential. The leaders who strike a balance between the two create conditions where people not only meet expectations, but also surpass them.

It begins with understanding your people and their dreams, struggles, and strengths. It's sitting down and saying, "I believe you can do even more. Here's what I see in you. Here's where you can grow. And here's how I'm going to support you in getting there." It's about being honest without being harsh. The magic happens when people know that you see potential and refuse to let them settle for less. When you coach from this place, feedback doesn't feel like criticism; it feels like an invitation to rise higher.

Coaching is a relationship, not a transaction. It's an ongoing balance of accountability and support. Great coaching changes more than performance metrics; it reshapes how people see themselves and strengthens their belief that their contributions matter. People don't give their best to a boss; they give it to a leader who challenges them with love.

Seasonality Curve: Navigating Renewal, Retention, and Release

You've seen it before: the employee who comes in on fire, excels in their role, uplifts the team, and demonstrates leadership in every interaction. Then, almost like flipping a switch, something changes. Performance declines, energy wanes, and the person you once depended on starts missing the mark. I call this the *Seasonality Curve*, a natural rhythm in people's lives and careers that mirrors the seasons we all experience. Just as nature cycles through seasons, people also move through similar phases in their work.

- Spring (a time for growth or renewal)
- Summer (momentum, when people hit their stride)
- Autumn (reflection and recalibration)
- Winter (confidence fades or life's challenges weigh heavily)

These shifts may be triggered by personal loss, burnout, or shifting priorities, and they can last for weeks, months, or even years. For leaders, the challenge is knowing how to respond when someone enters their Winter.

This is when leadership matters most. Some executives view holding onto an underperforming employee as a weakness, but wise leaders see it as a sign of discernment and maturity. Behind every dip is a human being, and often all they need is coaching, patience, or a spark to reignite their best self. Still, letting someone go is perhaps the most painful decision a leader can face, one that resonates through families, teams, and the broader culture. The Seasonality Curve invites us to see these cycles with compassion, to ask not just whether someone is failing today, but whether they can be guided toward renewal tomorrow. When you lead with that kind of perspective, you build loyalty and a culture strong enough to endure its own seasons.

At Dutch Bros, we used to say, "We love you on the way in and love you on the way out." Alex Oliva, one of our executives, once told me, "If someone decided to leave our company after a short time because they wanted to join a rock band, we'd buy them a guitar on their way out the door." That kind of care embodied what culture really means: honoring people at every stage of their career.

But even with love and care, every leader eventually faces the hard truth: someone who once thrived may no longer fit the culture you're trying to protect. Perhaps they've changed, perhaps the company has, or perhaps the values that once defined them have eroded under pressure. Whatever the reason, holding on past the point of fit helps no one: not the employee, not the team, and not the mission itself. The real test of leadership is knowing when to lean into renewal and when to release, and finding the courage to do both with humanity and compassion.

Ultimately, the Seasonality Curve is not about judging people; it's about stewarding culture. Renewal, retention, and release are all part of leadership's responsibility, just as seasons are part of nature's rhythm. Winter doesn't erase Spring; it prepares the ground for it. Letting someone go with dignity isn't failure; it's protecting the soil so new growth can flourish. And when your team sees you lead with fairness, compassion, and clarity in these moments, they gain confidence that the culture will endure no matter the season.

That's the legacy of the Seasonality Curve: reminding us that leadership is not just about building organizations, but about guiding people through their seasons with care, courage, and conviction.

Celebrate the Culture Carriers

An overlooked force in any company is the power of informal leaders. These are individuals who may not have formal titles but whose energy, consistency, and attitude influence the emotional climate around them daily. We call them the "culture carriers," and I've had the good fortune of working with many who fit that description throughout my career.

You've seen them too. They're the ones who arrive early because they want to set the tone for the day, bringing pastries, candy, or a game to entertain or challenge the team. They remember birthdays, check in when someone's having a rough day, and bring levity into high-pressure meetings, not to divert attention, but to make it more human. They lead without asking for recognition. They inspire without needing permission.

They are often the emotional center of a team, the stabilizers, the encouragers, the first to raise a hand when help is needed, and the last to ask for recognition. And what they offer is more than morale, it's momentum. A Gallup study demonstrates that having a close workplace friendship has a dramatic impact on employee engagement. Those who have a best friend at work are seven times more likely to be engaged in their jobs compared to those who don't.[46] That's not just social connection. That's someone acting as a relational anchor, which is exactly what culture carriers do on a large scale.

Culture carriers can be the reason someone stays at a company during tough times. Sometimes, they're the reason a new hire feels confident they made the right choice. Other times, they help shift a team away from cynicism and back toward hope. They're the ones who protect the culture from erosion, quietly, faithfully, and often without being asked. And in that way, they do more for the long-term health of an organization than any policy ever could.

That's why leaders must not only notice culture carriers but celebrate them publicly, specifically and consistently. Shine a light on the people who carry your culture forward, because they set the standard others will naturally rise to meet.

Culture is shaped in small, ordinary moments. The most powerful cultures aren't loud or flashy; they are steady, patient, and built through thousands of daily choices that, over time,

---

[46] Gallup. I have a best friend at work. Gallup: Engagement Resource Guide, January 19, 2024.
https://www.gallup.com/workplace/397058/increasing-importance -best-friend-work.aspx?

become second nature. As a leader or teammate, your most significant influence might not come from bold initiatives, but from the way you handle small moments: a calm word after tension, a handwritten note of thanks, or simply choosing to listen when it would be easier to walk away. Big wins are built on small acts. Enduring cultures are sustained by the everyday actions of people who choose to care in one moment at a time.

Every person helps shape culture, whether they intend to or not. And those who carry it with integrity remind the rest of us what it means to belong.

Spotlight: The Culture Carriers
Who they are:

- The steady voices when stress runs high
  - The encouragers who remember birthdays and small wins
  - The ones who model care without asking for credit

Why they matter:

- Anchor teams through tough seasons
  - Multiply trust and morale across the organization
- Protect culture in ways no policy or program ever can

How to lead them:

- Notice them
  - Celebrate them publicly
- Protect their influence as much as your bottom line

CHAPTER 10

Embracing the Hard Conversations

---

*"Accountability is a personal choice to rise above circum-
stances and demonstrate the ownership necessary for
achieving desired results."*
— Roger Connors, co-author of *The Oz Principle*

FAIR, FIRM & FRIENDLY

The Impact of a Leader

Jackie "Jack" Wayne Willingham was a leader of extraordinary strength, humility, and vision. He entered the U.S. Air Force during the Vietnam War, where he took on complex special assignments with quiet courage. Jack never glorifies his role, but he occasionally shares stories of his aircraft being "torn to shreds" during those final missions, a glimpse into the kind of resilience that defines his character. When he returned home, he didn't seek recognition; he sought purpose. His passion for engineering and construction became his new calling, a way to continue serving by shaping communities and creating spaces where people could gather and connect.

Over the next several decades, Jack left a lasting impact on the restaurant industry. He led with vision and skill at companies like Sambo's, Perkins, and later through his own venture, Wilcraft, before spending nearly twenty years as Senior Vice President of Construction and Design at CKE Restaurants. Jack had a rare ability to see opportunity where others saw problems. He could read a blueprint and not just envision a building but also imagine the people who would work there, the teams that would form inside it, and the communities it would serve. More than a builder of restaurants, Jack was a builder of people. His Christian faith guided him, his humility grounded him, and his conviction inspired those around him. He poured his heart into every project, leaving behind more than just buildings; he fostered a culture of learning, mentorship, and excellence. He never saw leadership as a title, but as a responsibility, one he carried with humility, humor, and a deep love for people.

What made Jack remarkable wasn't just what he accomplished, but how he led. He believed leadership was less about control and more about character; about showing up with heart. His philosophy became a compass for how I lead to this day, anchored in being Fair, Firm, and Friendly.

For me, and for many others, Jack's influence was life-changing. The professional world is undeniably better because he walked through it with integrity, vision, and love.

Fair, Firm, and Friendly

There's a myth that leadership means being tough, detached, and emotionally bulletproof. Showing too much of your heart makes you appear soft. That being friendly erodes your authority. That fairness is weakness. But the truth? Real leadership, the kind that builds loyalty and results, is rooted in being *Fair, Firm, and Friendly*.

That phrase wasn't pulled from a textbook. It was passed down to me by my late friend and mentor, Jack Willingham. He lived it. For him, "Fair, Firm, and Friendly" wasn't just a philosophy; it was about managing relationships effectively. Jack would say that business can be unforgiving, and you've got to be tough to succeed. But toughness doesn't mean abandoning conviction, compassion, or truth. For him, maintaining a strong character was nonnegotiable. This philosophy on how to treat others was his anchor.

In every negotiation, Jack expected the team to embrace all three cultural mindsets—Fair, Firm, and Friendly—not just one or two, but all three. It's a complete package. You need to be Fair enough to earn people's trust, Firm enough for your standards to hold weight, and Friendly enough that your team, vendors, suppliers, and colleagues feel comfortable approaching you. If you miss any one of these elements, things will start to fall apart. Be too fair and friendly without firmness? You'll be liked but not respected. Too firm without fairness? You'll rule through fear and foster silence instead of loyalty. And if you're friendly without standards? Congratulations, you've just started Club Chaos, and you're the DJ.

Remember that balance is everything. But relentless focus is key! When you get it right, and you lead with all three, something powerful happens, and you unlock the rare ability to lead with both love and results. That's the real sweet spot.

Fair

Fairness doesn't mean treating everyone the same. That shortcut only avoids hard choices. Genuine fairness involves treating people with equal respect while acknowledging that individuals have diverse needs, strengths, and circumstances. It requires clarity about expectations, transparency in feedback, and consistency in decision-making. Employees don't expect leaders to be perfect, but they do expect clarity and consistency. Jack modeled this by listening before judging and coaching with context, not assumptions.

In practice: Southwest Airlines has built decades of loyalty by embedding fairness into both its employee policies and customer-facing practices, including transparent communication and the absence of hidden fees. That commitment fostered consistency across the organization. Fairness integrated into daily decisions creates a stability that people can rely on.

Firm

On the other hand, being firm gets a bad rap because people often confuse it with control, intimidation, or micromanagement. But firmness, when done right, is about holding the line, defining who you are (as a person or a brand), modeling what is expected, and setting the boundaries on how your team is to be treated by others. It's saying, *"This is how we roll, and these are our standards. These are the lines we do not cross. And this is how we treat each other, and this is what matters here."* Being firm isn't about punishing mistakes but about protecting the culture you've worked so hard to build. Jack believed firmness defended the people doing it right and kept the mission from drifting.

In practice: Netflix is famous for its "freedom and responsibility" culture deck, but it's also famously firm about standards. The company has clear expectations: innovation is encouraged, but mediocrity has no place. That firmness ensures alignment while still leaving room for creativity.

Friendly
This is the practice that leaders often misunderstand. Friendly leadership is not a weakness; it's a strategy. When you're friendly, you shorten the distance between authority and build bridges that unlock honesty. When you are encouraging, people are more willing to take risks and stretch their potential. Gallup's research shows that employees who feel their manager genuinely cares about them as a person are significantly more engaged, productive, and less likely to leave their job. A friendly leader is not a pushover; a friendly leader is a powerhouse. They know that performance thrives when people feel valued, and encouragement is the fuel that drives it. They combine high standards with human connection, which creates lasting loyalty.

In practice: Costco has consistently outperformed its competitors not just through pricing, but also through its culture. Paying above-market wages, offering benefits, and treating employees with dignity built a loyal workforce. Their friendliness didn't weaken performance—it strengthened it, fueling retention and productivity.

> *"Culture is not the most important thing. It's the only thing."*
> —Jim Sinegal, Co-founder of Costco

Fair, Firm & Friendly is a leadership philosophy that encourages vulnerability wrapped in strength, accountability rooted in compassion, and relationships grounded in trust. When those three come together, leadership is at its best. But even with the right philosophy, there's still one constant threat: Ego.

Ego: The Silent Saboteur

Ego tends to slip in unnoticed, often showing up in whispers that sound reasonable: *"Protect yourself." "Make sure you're the smartest in the room." "Don't let anyone else get the credit."* Left unchecked, those whispers distort leadership into self-preservation instead of stewardship.

That's the quiet danger of ego, it feels like confidence but behaves like fear. It hides behind titles, metrics, and authority, convincing leaders they're serving the mission while subtly shifting the spotlight toward themselves. Over time, ego erodes what culture depends on most: trust. When people sense that recognition flows upward instead of outward, they stop giving their best. They pull back, giving less of themselves, because they feel undervalued. The light that once fueled creativity, collaboration, and courage starts to dim.

The irony is that when ego drives the decision, it feels powerful in the moment but weakens everything over time. Because ego doesn't build; it consumes. It devours credit, oxygen, and opportunity, leaving only compliance behind.

Research backs this up. A 2022 study published in *The Leadership Quarterly* found that leaders who exhibit higher levels of narcissism are more likely to create climates of fear and competition, leading to measurable declines in team performance and innovation (Nevicka et al., 2022)[47]. Conversely, a meta-analysis from the *Journal of Organizational Behavior* highlights that humble leadership, defined by openness,

---

[47] Nevicka, B., De Hoogh, A. H. B., Den Hartog, D. N., & Belschak, F. D. Narcissistic leaders: A review of current research and future directions. The Leadership Quarterly, 33(1), 101-112. 2022. https://doi.org/10.1016/j.leaqua.2021.101561

teachability, and acknowledgment of others, correlates strongly with higher engagement, psychological safety, and collaboration (Owens & Hekman, 2016). These findings reinforce what experience already tells us: ego isolates, but humility connects.[48]

The antidote is not passivity; it's presence. It's the kind of humility that doesn't minimize strength but channels it toward service. When leaders put mission over pride and people over position, they gain something far greater than authority; they gain loyalty.

That's why the fight against ego is never over. It's not a single moment of awareness but a daily discipline. Every meeting, every decision, every recognition moment is an invisible crossroads: *Is this about me, or is this about us?*

Leaders who choose "us" over "me" change everything. They create cultures where love and accountability coexist, where people feel seen, trusted, and inspired to do their best work. Authentic leadership doesn't need applause; it leaves an echo. It's quiet, steady, and deeply human. That's the heart of the *No EGO Policy*, a daily choice to serve, not self-preserve.

> *"True leadership is not about asserting authority, but about inspiring trust—being fair in your decisions, encouraging growth, and holding people accountable with kindness."*
> —Indra Nooyi, former CEO of PepsiCo

---

[48] Owens, B. P., & Hekman, D. R. How does leader humility influence team performance? Exploring the mechanisms of connection and collaboration. Journal of Organizational Behavior, 37(7), 957-978. 2016. https://doi.org/10.1002/job.2083

CHAPTER 11

Fueling the Fire Without Burning Out

"Fair isn't treating everyone the same. It's treating everyone with the same respect, while honoring their differences."

Speed Without a Compass

When Uber started, it felt like lightning in a bottle. It wasn't just a new way to get a ride; it was a revolution that changed how people viewed business itself. Internally, the company operated with the same energy it brought to the streets: relentless focus, big ambitions, and a rough-and-tumble culture that celebrated hustle above all else. If you were hungry enough, smart enough, and willing to push limits, Uber offered the ride of a lifetime.

And for a while, it seemed to work. The culture gave people room to push boundaries and think ten steps ahead of everyone else. The company grew rapidly, raising billions and disrupting industries in every major city worldwide. But the very mentality that fueled its rise also planted the seeds of its decline. Beneath all that speed, something more fragile was being overlooked: values.

Winning wasn't enough; it had to be domination at any cost. Crushing competitors wasn't just a strategy; it was Uber's identity. In that environment, ethical shortcuts became acceptable. Then expected, and eventually, normalized.

The culture, once exhilarating, turned exhausting. As the company expanded, toxic leadership behaviors went unchecked. Aggression was praised. Empathy and accountability were seen as liabilities. There was no time to pause, no room for vulnerability. Ruthlessness was mistaken for excellence, and risk-taking shifted from bold to reckless. What once felt disruptive started to seem dangerous. Because leadership never clearly defined boundaries, there was no shared understanding of what was acceptable and what wasn't. Culture became a byproduct of performance, not its foundation. That's where the breakdown began.

People began to leave not because the mission had changed, but because the culture had. The ground shifted beneath them.

Then came the headlines, followed by lawsuits and investigations. By the time the company attempted to course-correct, the damage was already evident. The very culture that once gave Uber an advantage had become its most significant liability.

Uber's story serves as a cautionary tale. When a company grows faster than its values, its culture begins to break down under pressure. Uber didn't falter because it lacked ideas or market presence—it faltered because it failed to protect the integrity that sustains growth.

Beyond the Hustle: Building Sustainable Momentum

Companies that endure are not the ones sprinting for short-term wins; they're the ones mastering the marathon. Longevity demands leaders, teams, and the culture itself to pace themselves for the road ahead. People don't lose their love for the mission because the work is hard; they lose it when the work feels disconnected from meaning. Therefore, businesses must maintain momentum by offering people something worth running toward.

Somewhere along the way, hustle culture got glorified. We've all heard the slogans: "Rise and grind." "No days off." "Sleep when you're dead." It sounds bold and edgy, but it's a blueprint for burnout. Over time, small mistakes multiply, creativity fades, and the same employees who once lit up the room now drag themselves through the day. Meetings lose energy, conversations become transactional, and what once inspired starts to feel exhausting.

Research reinforces this idea: momentum in organizations isn't simply about speed or constant activity. Genuine momentum combines direction, endurance, and adaptability, traits that help teams move forward without breaking down (Wiebe et al., 2012). Cultures that balance high performance with purpose and recovery avoid burnout and instead develop lasting power. As Pacheco (2025) notes in the Harvard Business Review, sustainable organizations are those that "align cultural values with long-term strategy," ensuring that employees' energy isn't only spent but continually replenished. True staying power isn't about glorifying exhaustion, but fostering a culture where people are motivated to maintain excellence, even as seasons change and challenges arise.

A Tale of Two Paths: Hustle Versus Endurance

We don't need to look far for examples of how culture can make or break a company.

WeWork famously embodied hustle culture, encouraging all-night work sessions, glorifying "always on" energy, and building a brand on rapid expansion.[49] At first, it looked like unstoppable momentum. The company raised billions, grew at lightning speed, and captured the imagination of entrepreneurs and investors worldwide. But as hype overtook culture, the very energy that fueled growth became unsustainable. Employees burned out, turnover soared, and leadership missteps eroded commitment, making what was once revolutionary feel reckless.

Patagonia offers the opposite story. For decades, they've built a culture on valuing rest, balance, and connection to purpose.[50] Employees are encouraged to surf when the waves are good, and shops are closed for the holidays, allowing people to spend time with their families. Rooted in its mission to minimize environmental impact, Patagonia has cultivated a culture

[49] Cusumano, C. How WeWork went from a $47 billion valuation to bankruptcy in under 5 years. Business Insider, October 14, 2021. https://www.businessinsider.com/how-wework-went-bankrupt-rise-fall-history-2021-10

[50] Patagonia. Earth is now our only shareholder. Patagonia, September 14, 2022. https://www.patagonia.com/ownership

of balance and long-term purpose. The result is a culture of endurance, where purpose renews itself year after year.

Other companies have found their own versions of this sustainable rhythm. W. L. Gore & Associates removed rigid hierarchies, allowing leadership to emerge organically, fostering autonomy, and building accountability through peer-to-peer relationships.

W. L. Gore & Associates demonstrates yet another path to resilience: autonomy. By removing rigid hierarchies and allowing leadership to emerge where needed, teams self-organize, decisions arise from collaboration rather than command, and employees take ownership of the outcomes. The result is a culture that adapts quickly, proving that empowerment can be as powerful a driver of endurance as values or structure.

HubSpot underscores the role of rest as a strategic advantage. Through practices like its "Week of Rest" and "No Internal Meeting Fridays," the company has built intentional recovery into its culture. These rhythms protect creative energy, prevent burnout, and sustain engagement. HubSpot's people-first approach shows that cultures designed with recovery in mind don't just feel better–they perform better, because energy is preserved for the moments it's needed most.[51]

But endurance isn't only about values, it's also about structure. Affirm demonstrates this in a remote-first environment where face-to-face interaction is rare. Instead of leaving culture to chance, Affirm designs it with intention: balancing flexibility with clear expectations and quarterly in-person gatherings. These rhythms prevent disconnection and ensure that performance and culture move forward together. As their leadership puts it, the goal of coming together isn't just to overlap

---

[51] People Staff. HubSpot: A culture that puts people first. People, August 8, 2024. https://people.com/human-interest-people-100-companies-that-care-7749999

on tasks but to strengthen shared identity and belonging.[52] Affirm demonstrates that even in distributed models, culture and high performance can coexist when trust and structure are aligned.

The lesson is clear. Hustle can give you headlines, but it rarely gives you heritage. The companies people admire decades later, such as Disney, Trader Joe's, and Costco, aren't remembered for grinding employees down. They're remembered for creating environments where people's energy and love for the mission can last a lifetime. Success that endures is momentum that compounds, not adrenaline that crashes.

Meaningful Milestones

"The way your employees feel is the way your customers will feel. If your employees don't feel valued, neither will your customers."
—Sybil F. Stershic

Culture isn't a finish line; it's the heartbeat of the organization, the steady pulse that keeps people aligned and energized. The challenge isn't just creating energy but sustaining it without burning people out. That requires intention: designing an environment where progress feels purposeful and wins restore people instead of depleting them.

The best leaders understand that momentum isn't about speed; it's about meaning. They create *meaningful milestones* that matter, checkpoints that re-anchor the team to the mission and remind them why the effort is worth it. Without those moments, even the most committed people lose sight of the bigger picture. Recognition at the finish line alone is too late; by then, fatigue has already stolen energy and creativity.

---

[52] Business Insider. Affirm is proving that a remote-first culture can still be high performance. Business Insider, December 11, 2024. https://www.businessinsider.com/affirm-remote-first-culture-2024-12

Meaningful milestones don't need to be grand. They are intentional checkpoints that say: "We see you. We appreciate you. We're doing this together." When you celebrate smartly, you re-anchor your team to the mission. You remind them why the early mornings, tough conversations, and late-night problem-solving sessions are worth it. It's essential to celebrate significant milestones, product launches, record sales, and the opening of new locations, but the smaller victories matter just as much. A breakthrough idea in a meeting, a process that finally clicks, or a new hire finding their stride can carry equal weight in sustaining momentum. The best leaders learn to spot and elevate these quieter wins because they compound over time. This is a muscle leaders must deliberately exercise, retraining the brain to notice moments that aren't always visible at first glance. The more you practice spotting small victories, the more you'll learn to appreciate your team, each individual contribution, and even the daily rhythm of progress. Over time, this doesn't just shape how you lead; it reshapes how you see the world, giving you a healthier outlook on both your work and personal life. Small wins add up to build confidence, turning ordinary weeks into meaningful chapters of a larger story.

When people see progress, they feel a sense of momentum. Not perfection, but progress. And energy is emotional before it becomes operational. People need to see wins along the way, not just the final finish line that's months or years out. When employees feel like they're winning, they show up like winners. When they feel invisible, the spark dims, even if the work still gets done. Leaders play a crucial role in removing obstacles, setting clear goals, and creating an environment that allows teams to move quickly without unnecessary friction. They create conditions that foster momentum.

That's why recognition isn't a perk; it's a discipline. Momentum is as much about emotional intelligence as it is about strategy, knowing when to push, when to pause, and when to celebrate. Recognition doesn't need to be flashy to be effective. Often, it's the small, authentic touches—such as a handwritten note, a story shared in a team huddle, or a personal thank-you—that carry the most weight.

As Matt Phelan wrote in *The Happiness Index* (2022), recognition is a fundamental human need. People want to know their work matters and contributes to a greater purpose. [53] That's why effective recognition is both instinctive and intentional. Simple comments like, "What you said was brilliant," can make a significant impact. It's tailored to the individual to ensure it truly resonates, grounded in authenticity, and built into the daily fabric of the culture. When organizations embed recognition into onboarding, team rituals, and leadership habits, they build more than momentum; they cultivate a culture where people feel valued from the very beginning.

Emotions at Work in Culture

When leaders celebrate meaningfully, they do more than elevate morale; they reinforce resilience, loyalty, and a shared sense of progress. Recognition signals to the team that their efforts matter and that their work is advancing the mission.

Howard M. Weiss and Russell Cropanzano's Affective Events Theory (1996) helps explain why workplace culture is shaped less by sweeping policies and more by the accumulation of everyday moments.[54] The theory centers on how specific workplace events, both positive and negative, can trigger emotional reactions that impact job satisfaction, performance, and overall engagement. What makes AET particularly relevant is

---

[53] Phelan, Matt. "Recognition (Acknowledgement)." The Happiness Index, September 12, 2022. https://thehappinessindex.com/blog/neuroscience-recognition/

[54] Weiss, H. M., & Cropanzano, R. Affective Events Theory: A theoretical discussion of the structure, causes and consequences of affective experiences at work. In B. M. Staw & L. L. Cummings (Eds.), Research in Organizational Behavior (Vol. 18, pp. 1-74). JAI Press, 1996.

its recognition of a feedback loop: how one event's emotional response can influence how employees interpret subsequent events, shaping their connection to your mission over time.

It's not just broad job characteristics that influence how people feel at work, but also everyday workplace experiences and interpersonal moments that shape employee emotions and, in turn, their job performance. These factors build or erode engagement over time. Practically, AET reminds leaders that culture resides in the in-between, the moments and memories formed between missions and metrics. It conveys a simple yet powerful message: every interaction matters, and consistent kindness, clarity, and attention create emotional momentum that can become a cultural asset or liability.

We can clearly see this dynamic in Microsoft's cultural transformation under Satya Nadella. When Nadella became CEO in 2014, Microsoft was viewed as stagnant, defined more by internal rivalries than the lack of invention.[55] Nadella shifted the culture by encouraging a "growth mindset," embedding recognition into the way teams collaborated. He made it clear that progress wasn't just measured in quarterly results, but in how employees learned, shared, and encouraged one another. By celebrating small wins and modeling humility at the top, Nadella reignited momentum, restored employee pride, and positioned Microsoft at the forefront of the tech industry once again. The turnaround wasn't powered by slogans or hustle—it was sustained through intentional recognition and a culture that valued progress over ego.

That's why guarding momentum is just as important as building it. One great quarter doesn't guarantee the next. Momentum, once gained, is fragile. It's like a fire you've built with your own

[55] Prakash, D., Bisla, J., & Rastogi, Y. Leadership strategies of Satya Nadella: A review of extant literature. International Journal of Research & Innovation in Social Science, 5(1), 785-794. 2021. https://doi.org/10.47772/IJRISS.2025.914MG0062

hands, glowing brightly, providing warmth, and illuminating the way forward. But if you walk away too soon or become complacent, that fire can flicker and die out faster than you ever imagined. You must remain vigilant, hungry and humble. That's your call to action. Momentum can die from a thousand little cuts, like tolerating bad attitudes, ignoring early warning signs, or believing that results alone are enough to keep a team motivated.

Guarding the gains means staying anchored in the fundamentals: clear communication, thoughtful recognition, intentional coaching, deep listening, and a steady return to purpose. Momentum never moves in a straight line; it loops, dips, and surges. High-performing cultures accept this rhythm. They recognize that slowdowns are not disasters, but checkpoints and signals to recalibrate and re-engage.

That's not failure. That's being human. People get tired, markets shift, and seasons change. The danger isn't the slowdown; it's how you respond to it. Many leaders treat the dip like a disaster, but great leaders don't panic when the pace changes. They pause, step back, and zoom out to create space for renewal. By treating dips as part of the natural cycle rather than signs of failure, they protect the team and keep them aligned. When you see the slowdown as part of the rhythm, not the end of the road, you give your team the clarity and space to move forward, faster, wiser, and stronger, leading to growth and lasting success.

Few companies illustrate this better than Netflix.[56] What initially appeared to be a decline in its core DVD business became the catalyst for one of the most successful reinventions in modern business history. Netflix didn't cling to its past; it saw the slowdown as a sign to evolve. In 2007, it launched

---

[56] Strategyzer. Netflix is winding down its DVD-by-mail service for good. Strategyzer Insights, August 30, 2023. https://www.strategyzer.com/library/netflix-is-winding-down-its-dvd-by-mail-service-for-good

its streaming service ("Watch Now"), gradually moving away from physical media to digital delivery. That move was risky, bandwidth was inconsistent, and consumer habits weren't yet fully developed; however, Netflix invested early, betting that the future of entertainment lay in streaming, not shipping. Over time, streaming became the majority of its revenue, and by 2023, the DVD-by-mail service was finally retired after twenty-five years. This transition wasn't driven by desperation; it was driven by vision, data, and an unrelenting focus on staying relevant.

What makes Netflix a powerful case study is how it utilized meaningful milestones throughout the transition. From its first online streaming titles to producing original content (like *House of Cards* in 2013), the company consistently recognized smaller wins within bigger shifts. Each pivot, subscription model, streaming, and original content was anchored with signals that progress was absolute, forward motion was sustainable, and the team's work mattered. This ability to respond to dips with renewal, rather than fear, set the foundation for Netflix's staying power in a highly competitive market.

Refueling the Fire

When that slowdown becomes noticeable, it's the leader's cue to reconnect the team to the purpose behind the work: why it matters, why it's worth doing, and why the effort is still worthwhile. Share the stories that once sparked belief. Clear out the friction, the blockers, and the unnecessary complexities that drain energy. Endurance, not endless hustle, defines the healthiest cultures. They know how to re-center, reset, and rise again.

Think of momentum like an engine. When it sputters, you don't throw the car away; you tune it. Momentum isn't lost forever. It just needs attention, intention, and a fresh spark.

First, bring back clarity. In times of fatigue or drift, ambiguity creeps in like fog. People start guessing what matters, who's responsible, or where they're headed. That's the moment to anchor back to purpose. Restate the mission. Paint the destination vividly. Remind your team why they initially signed up for the experience.

Second, lower the hurdles. Teams often lose steam because complexity has crept in. Meetings multiply. Processes swell. Approvals pile up. What once felt fast now feels bogged down by red tape. Great leaders ask, *"What's getting in your way?"*—and then they listen and act, clearing the path so progress feels possible again.

Third, celebrate progress, not just perfection. Big wins deserve the spotlight, but momentum is sustained by the accumulation of small victories: a new hire finding their stride, a store bouncing back from a tough month, or a customer relationship turning a corner. Each one is fuel. Recognize it, cheer it, and make it visible.

Fourth, bring genuine energy. Culture needs leaders who show up with authenticity, resilience, and hope, especially in hard times. Energy is contagious. If leaders appear cynical, the team will likely mirror that attitude. But when leaders are steady, curious, and committed to the mission, that attitude spreads faster than fear.

Finally, put people first. Processes and plans matter, but momentum lives in human hearts. Take time to check in, not just for metrics, but for meaning. Go on a gratitude tour. Show your team members that they matter beyond their performance. When employees feel seen and valued, they lean back in, and the culture finds its spark again.

That's the moment, sometimes so subtle you almost miss it, when momentum stops feeling like a push and starts feeling like a pull. That's when you know you've moved from chasing success to building something bigger than yourself. That's how movements are born. Movements happen when people don't just show up because they have to, but because they want to. They expand upon the mission, contributing their own ideas and inviting others in. Movements can't be forced; they can only be earned.

These practices aren't just theory. Southwest Airlines offers a powerful example. Their legendary "LUV culture" has thrived for decades because leaders continually refuel the fire by reconnecting employees to purpose, simplifying processes, and celebrating people. From handwritten notes of appreciation to companywide recognition of front-line staff, Southwest makes momentum personal. Even in turbulent times, they've shown that when employees feel loved and valued, they carry that energy to customers, turning an airline into a movement.

And movements thrive when leaders know how to step out of the spotlight and let the team shine, when celebrations are peer-to-peer as much as top-down, when ideas bubble up from every corner, and when love and leadership are so deeply woven into the fabric of the workplace that they cannot be separated.

You'll know you've built a movement when your people start saying: *"We're family here." "This place changed my life." "I tell everyone they should come work here."* Those aren't recruitment slogans. They are badges of honor your team gives you—and they can't be faked.

Movements aren't loud because leaders demand it. They're loud because love demands it.

If there's one lesson to carry from this chapter, it's this: culture isn't something you set and forget. Culture is a daily decision to show up with humility, with clarity, and with fierce love for the people around you. With every conversation, every policy, and every moment you choose curiosity over judgment or grace over frustration, you shape the culture in which you work.

When you treat culture as the living organism it is, feeding it, tending to it, and adjusting it, you'll see it return the favor. It will feed your results, fuel your brand, and multiply your leadership impact beyond anything you could accomplish alone. Most importantly, it will make the business, the brand, and the community you're building feel like it genuinely means something.

Because it does, and when you lead with love, you have the privilege of being the architect of that meaning, building not just a culture, but a movement that endures.

CHAPTER 12

Creating the Right Infrastructure

"Work is no longer about offices. It's about people. Belonging, connection, and shared purpose can exist anywhere—if we build them with care."
—Satya Nadella, CEO of Microsoft

Never Let Go

Disney's hug rule, or the "no-let-go-first" rule, requires that characters never end a hug with a child until the child lets go first.[57] *This hug rule has become so iconic that it's rumored to trace back to Walt Disney's own belief: "You never know how much that child may need that hug." Whether formalized in training or adopted organically, the directive captures what Disney culture is all about: emotional resonance, attention to small but meaningful details, and unwavering guest focus.*[58]

The origin of the rule is simple yet powerful. By allowing a child to linger in a heartfelt embrace, Disney ensures each guest feels like they are a part of something magical. It's an emotional anchor—a tangible act of kindness that says, "I'm here for you, whenever you need me." This kind of ritual isn't just about hugging; it's a master class in designing culture through experience.

That hug exemplifies Disney's broader operational rigor. Characters are meticulously trained: no sunglasses indoors, no visible tattoos, no breaking the illusion. Every interaction, each smile, each gesture, is calibrated to strengthen the magic. In training staff to follow procedures as seemingly minor as a hug, Disney reinforces a single overarching message: culture is in the details.

By translating significant values—such as care, presence, and authenticity—into precise behavior, Disney creates a consistent emotional experience that feels genuine across every

---

[57] Inside the Magic. "Disney's "Hug Rule" Completely Changes Character Experience." Inside the Magic, January 2024.

[58] Sinclair Broadcast Group. "Disney's 'Hug Rule' You Need to Know About." Adelaidenow, March 26, 2024. https://www.adelaidenow.com.au/lifestyle/the-disney-hug-rule-you-need-to-know-about/news-story/677a11fb7773d1d437e355c474ef6d3e?utm_source

interaction. The hug rule shows that slogans don't define company culture, but by the small, thoughtful moments that connect people and reinforce purpose. That's why it screams culture: it's the perfect expression of a philosophy rooted in empathy, experience, and intentional design.

Disney's practice offers a template for any organization seeking to translate values into action. When leaders operationalize cultural ideals through scripts, training, or norms, they create reliability and emotional cohesion. In essence, they make culture palpable. That is authentic cultural leadership: ensuring every individual interaction becomes a living testament to your core beliefs, and that those beliefs become embedded in the day-to-day experiences that define your brand.

NOTE: *Check out your favorite social media service to see examples of this in action (but be prepared to grab a tissue).*

Loyalty Starts on the Inside

It's easy to talk about customer service as the front line of business, but what most leaders miss is that excellent service is a byproduct, not a starting point. The fundamental foundation of customer loyalty is employee engagement. Employees must love the company before customers ever will. The relationship between employees and the company sets the tone for every subsequent customer interaction that follows. If people on the inside feel proud of where they work, that pride ripples outward.

Small acts of service, like a smile, a longer-than-usual phone call, or a quick problem-solving gesture, aren't listed in job descriptions. They're a reflection of someone who believes in what they do. Research shows that something as simple as a genuine smile can significantly improve customer mood and satisfaction, building loyalty in ways policies alone never could (Otterbring, 2017; Hennig-Thurau et al., 2006).[59]

The Ritz-Carlton built its world-class reputation on this very principle. Their famous motto, "Ladies and gentlemen serving ladies and gentlemen," isn't just a slogan; it's a daily expectation that every employee, from housekeeping to the front desk, has both the dignity and the authority to create extraordinary moments for guests.[60] That's why a housekeeper might hand-write a note to welcome a child with their favorite stuffed animal, or a server will go out of their way to remember a guest's preference. Those small, unscripted actions embody belief in the mission, and they're what guests remember long after checkout.

Zappos is often cited as a benchmark, and for good reason. From the outside, it's a customer service machine. But internally, it's built on something more powerful: trust. Employees aren't handed scripts; they're given freedom. There's no time limit on calls. In fact, one internal record shows a Zappos customer-service representative spent ten hours and forty-three minutes on a single call with a customer, illustrating how deeply the company values genuine connection over speed.[61] Some

[59] Otterbring, T. Smile for a while: The effect of employee-displayed smiling on customer affect and satisfaction. Journal of Service Management, 28(2), 284-304. 2017. https://doi.org/10.1108/JOSM-11-2015-0372; Hennig-Thurau, T., Groth, M., Paul, M., & Gremler, D. D. Are all smiles created equal? How emotional contagion and emotional labor affect service relationships. Journal of Marketing, 70(3), 58-73. 2006. https://doi.org/10.1509/jmkg.70.3.58

[60] The Ritz-Carlton Leadership Center. Foundations of our brand. https://ritzcarltonleadershipcenter.com/about-us/about-us-foundations-of-our-brand/; Perna, G. (2019, March 26). Ritz-Carlton founder Horst Schulze on creating a gold standard. Chief Executive, March 26, 2019. https://chiefexecutive.net/ritz-carlton-founder-horst-schulze-gold-standard/2/

[61] Feloni, R. A Zappos employee had the company's longest customer-service call at 10 hours, 43 minutes. Business Insider, July 26, 2016. https://www.businessinsider.com/zappos-employee-sets-record-for-longest-customer-service-call-2016-7

reps have even driven across town to fulfill orders themselves. These aren't gimmicks. They're the natural output of a company that rewards care, celebrates autonomy, and believes service is a human act, not a metric.

What Zappos proves is that extraordinary customer experiences don't happen by accident; they're the result of a culture designed to empower people. So how do you build that kind of culture? Start by recognizing that engaged employees produce not just more work, but also better work.[62] That extra time, that extra effort, becomes a form of capital. It frees up your team to spend more energy on service, not just survival. Engagement doesn't just lift morale; it expands capacity.

This higher productivity is also reflected in improved quality, with fewer errors, stronger customer interactions, and more effective execution. Motivated employees don't just meet expectations; they surpass them, driven by belief rather than obligation. And this isn't theory; it's consistently proven in practice: Gallup's 2020 meta-analysis of employee engagement found that companies in the top quartile of engagement report 21 percent higher profitability, 17 percent higher productivity, 24 to 59 percent lower turnover, and 41 percent lower absenteeism compared to those in the bottom quartile.[63] Gallup's 2023 State of the Global Workplace report further reinforced this, noting that only 23 percent of employees worldwide are engaged. Yet, those who are highly involved drive substantially stronger performance and well-being outcomes.[64] The message is clear: engage-

---

[62] Korn Ferry. "Workforce 2025: Power Shifts". Korn Ferry Hay Group Global Study, 2020.

[63] Gallup. Employee engagement meta-analysis: 10th edition. Gallup, Inc.,2020.https://www.gallup.com/workplace/336941/employee-engagement-meta-analysis.aspx

[64] Gallup.Stateoftheglobalworkplace:2023report.Gallup,Inc.,2023. https://www.gallup.com/workplace/349484/state-of-the-global-workplace.aspx

ment translates directly into improved output and business health. Building and maintaining a culture that fosters engagement doesn't just improve the work environment; it fuels performance, loyalty, and long-term growth. For leaders, this is a strategic imperative.

When employees feel like they're investing their time in something meaningful, rather than wasting it on tasks disconnected from purpose, everything changes. This is what researchers Greg Oldham and Richard Hackman called *task significance*: the feeling that your work has a real impact on others.[65] It's not just about job satisfaction; it's about identity and contribution. And when employees feel that their company is a force for good in their own lives, they naturally extend that goodness outward to the customer.

You don't need to become a gamified tech company to create a culture that feels energizing. But you do need to be intentional. Fun, recognition, shared wins, and daily moments of connection all add up. When employees feel like they're playing for something bigger than themselves, your culture becomes your competitive edge. And your customers will feel it long before they ever see your mission statement.

> *"People rarely succeed unless they have fun in what they are doing."*
>
> —Dale Carnegie

The Culture Wars: Remote Versus In-Office Isn't the Real Battle

The real question isn't just how to engage employees; it's where and under what conditions that engagement can thrive.

---

[65] Oldham, Greg R., and J. Richard Hackman. "Work Redesign". Addison-Wesley Publishing Company, 1980.

For nearly thirty years of my career, I've worked in remote or hybrid settings shaped by the demands of each role. At Hunsaker & Associates, I spent a significant amount of time outside the office, obtaining permits and collaborating directly with government agencies, stakeholders, and community partners. At McDonald's, hybrid work took on new meaning, and construction sites required a "boots on the ground" presence, where accountability depended on a firsthand understanding of schedules, craft, and budgets.

That same dynamic expanded at CKE Restaurants, where accountability extended beyond the brand to franchise partners. Balancing these responsibilities across a franchise organization meant acting as a tactician, enforcer, and resource all at once, ensuring projects were delivered to brand standards while employing a common-sense approach to quality, cost, and execution. Dunkin' Brands demanded the same discipline, and later at Dutch Bros, the model scaled even further. Growing the brand and building the team gave me the chance to bring in exceptional talent from across the country, and together we achieved significant success. We achieved this by leveraging proven tools and practices from several pioneers, including Microsoft, GitLab, HubSpot, and others, while adapting them to our own culture and growth strategy.

The debate over remote versus in-office work continues to divide leaders. Remote work clearly offers flexibility, autonomy, and often improved well-being. A 2022 Gallup study found that employees with hybrid or remote options reported higher engagement and lower burnout than those working entirely on-site.[66] Since engagement has a strong correlation with productivity, remote and hybrid models can, in fact, boost performance.

---

[66] Gallup. "State of the Global Workplace 2022 Report". Gallup, August 31, 2022. https://www.gallup.com/workplace/349484/state-of-the-global-workplace.aspx

Yet, the picture isn't without complexity. Microsoft's 2023 Work Trend Index revealed that 85 percent of leaders feel less confident about employee productivity and connection in hybrid work environments (Microsoft, 2023).[67] The disconnect lies less in the capability of employees than in the perception of leaders. Higher engagement points to strong potential, but leaders can feel uncertain about whether productivity is truly being realized.

What often gets overlooked is the role of accountability. Many leaders still equate presence with productivity, assuming that if people are in the office, they're automatically contributing. But accountability isn't about proximity; it's about clarity, expectations, and consistent follow-through. A team with strong accountability rhythms, clear goals, transparent metrics, and regular feedback can thrive regardless of location.

GitLab, as one of the world's largest all-remote companies, with over 2,000 employees across more than sixty countries, has proven that structure and accountability can replace physical presence. They utilize publicly available dashboards and handbooks that document nearly every process, expectation, and decision, ensuring transparency to both their peers and leadership. This radical visibility means that no one is left guessing about priorities or performance; employees can hold themselves and each other accountable in real time. Weekly check-ins, asynchronous updates, and clearly defined project ownership provide accountability without micromanagement. Instead of assuming productivity through visibility, GitLab demonstrates how distributed teams can stay aligned, trusted, and productive at scale, while sharing in agreed-upon deliverables. Their model shows that with the proper rituals, remote work doesn't weaken culture; it strengthens it by

---

[67] Microsoft. "2023 Work Trend Index: Annual Report". March 8, 2023. https://www.microsoft.com/en-us/worklab/work-trend-index/2023

forcing leaders to clarify expectations and empower teams to own results (GitLab, 2021).[68]

The same principles apply during moments of global distraction. Consider the World Cup: some organizations resist flexibility, while others embrace it by letting employees adjust their schedules to watch matches. Neuroscience shows that multitasking reduces focus and increases errors; people are more effective when they can fully engage in the event and then return recharged. Companies that adapt to these moments earn trust and develop goodwill. *The Happiness Index* highlights that consistent flexibility fosters well-being through trust, balance, and autonomy–drivers that fuel both happiness and productivity (The Happiness Index, 2023).[69]

Hybrid work, when thoughtfully designed, offers the best of both worlds. Owl Labs' 2021 State of Remote Work report found that 90 percent of employees were as productive or more productive working remotely, with 84 percent reporting greater happiness. One in three workers said they would quit if remote options were taken away, illustrating that flexibility has become a condition of engagement (Owl Labs, 2021).[70] At the same time, many workers still crave face-to-face connections. The best leaders don't see this as a contradiction; they intentionally design hybrid structures, setting clear in-office days for collaboration and preserving remote flexibility for deep work.

---

[68] GitLab. "The Remote Playbook: Lessons from GitLab, the World's Largest All-Remote Company." GitLab, 2021. https://about.gitlab.com/company/culture/all-remote/.
[69] Whitehead-Smith, Elle. "Flexibility Is for Life – Not Just the World Cup." The Happiness Index, November 22, 2022, https://thehappinessindex.com/blog/flexibility-world-cup/
[70] Owl Labs. "State of Remote Work 2021." Owl Labs, 2021. https://www.owllabs.com/state-of-remote-work/2021

This balance is becoming a decisive advantage in today's talent market. The U.S. Chamber of Commerce (2023)[71] reported that millions of open jobs exist with too few workers to fill them, particularly in healthcare, construction, and technology. Companies like H-E-B have defied shortages by investing in career development and employee well-being, building loyalty in a competitive labor market (H-E-B, 2022).[72] *HubSpot* went further, redesigning its entire employee experience around flexibility and belonging, with rituals like "No Internal Meeting Fridays" and a "work from anywhere" policy. The result? Engagement soared (HubSpot, 2022).[73]

The lesson is clear: the future of work isn't about remote versus in-office work, it's about culture as infrastructure. Companies that cling to outdated models will continue to lose top talent. At the same time, those that anchor their culture in flexibility, trust, and accountability will reduce costly turnover and remain resilient, attracting the people they need most. In a labor market that is rewriting the rules, culture is the decisive advantage.

---

[71] U.S. Chamber of Commerce. "The State of the American Workforce." U.S. Chamber of Commerce, 2023. https://www.uschamber.com/workforce.

[72] H-E-B. "H-E-B Corporate Responsibility Report." H-E-B, 2022. https://www.heb.com/static-page/corporate-responsibility.

[73] HubSpot. "Culture Code." HubSpot, 2022. https://www.hubspot.com/culture.

CHAPTER 13

Steering the Soul of Your Business Back Home

"A company's culture is the foundation for future innovation. An entrepreneur's job is to build the foundation."
—Brian Chesky, Airbnb

Do You Bleed Ketchup?

My first authentic experience in the QSR industry was working at a McDonald's in San Clemente as a teenager. Some twenty years later, I was back, this time fresh into a new role as an Area Construction Manager for the McDonald's corporate office in San Diego, reporting to Don Ikeler. I was immersed in a world that blended precision, scale, and an unmistakable sense of pride, and a culture that was a unique blend of talent and diversity; it felt deeply personal.

One phrase, casually exchanged in meetings, caught my attention early: "Do you bleed ketchup?" I thought it was a joke at first, some sort of McDonald-ism meant to lighten the mood. But it wasn't long before I recognized its weight. It was a sort of litmus test. A way of asking: Are you genuinely committed to the brand? Are you emotionally and professionally invested in the mission? Do you care enough to obsess over every detail, to protect the brand like it's your own, and to give more than what's required, because it matters?

That saying, as it turns out, had deeper roots. The earliest documented reference appeared in a 2005 Prague Tribune article, noting that McDonald's founder Ray Kroc believed a franchisee needed to have "ketchup in their veins" or, as others would rephrase it, be "bleeding ketchup" to thrive in the business. In that context, the phrase wasn't about nostalgia or corporate folklore; it was about full-hearted allegiance to a system, a standard, and a shared vision of excellence. It meant taking pride in the Golden Arches.

And people did. McDonald's, back then (and even today), is among the most sought-after innovators in the industry. From architecture and development to the operational execution inside the shop, the commitment was visceral. During my tenure, the occasional visit from Joan Kroc carried an unspoken reminder that McDonald's wasn't just a business; it was a legacy. One built on consistency, discipline, a love of the system, and an unwavering belief that each crew member and every leader had a responsibility to one another and to meet customer needs to make the most significant impact on the business.

At the time, I didn't realize how formative that environment would be. I was young, eager, maybe a little out of my depth, but I wanted to earn that badge of honor. I was slowly learning to bleed ketchup.

Looking back, that question, "Do you bleed ketchup?" was more than cultural shorthand. It lived in the way people showed up, took pride in the process, and understood that excellence was everyone's job; it was about heart. It revealed a powerful truth: believe in what you're building and who you're creating it with, and everything else will fall into place.

The Hidden Threat: Culture Drift

You've built a strong culture, assembled a trustworthy team, and created a company people are proud to be part of. Now comes the real challenge: keeping the fire alive without accidentally burning the house down. Because here's the truth that catches even the best leaders off guard: momentum is powerful, but unmanaged momentum can be dangerous.

As leaders, developing people is only half the challenge. The other half involves shaping, safeguarding, and evolving the culture in which those people live and work. Committed leaders wake up and choose culture every day because they understand one thing others often miss: consistency outperforms charisma every time. Culture isn't something you set and forget; it's something you fight for, nurture, and grow alongside your team, especially during storms.

Great cultures remain strong because leaders notice the drift early and steer people back to the original mission with humility and hope. Resetting culture isn't a failure; it's a leadership opportunity. It's a reminder that every day, we're either moving closer to the culture we envision or drifting further away from it. And here's the beauty: even when the culture falters, its core remains. You just need to reignite the spark and be brave enough to bring it home again.

Even the strongest companies can see their culture drift. It's not because anyone intended for it to happen, but because culture, like anything alive, requires constant care. Perhaps growth occurred faster than expected, or a few key hires didn't work out as planned. Perhaps leadership was stretched too thin and stopped exemplifying the behaviors that formed the foundation. Whatever the cause, it's not the slip that defines you; it's how you respond.

Bad people don't break cultures. They're worn down by good people who lose clarity, connection, or conviction along the way. If you sense the culture slipping, pause, breathe, and then rally. Bring your team together, acknowledge the shift openly. Don't sugarcoat it, but don't overthink it either. Name what you're seeing, remind everyone what you're fighting for, and, most importantly, invite them to help rebuild the culture. You can even transform it into something more substantial. People want to be enlisted, not lectured into caring about the business.

Many world-class organizations experience dips in engagement. They can encounter fatigue or boredom because change is typically cyclical, not linear. Research by Richard Boyatzis and colleagues on Intentional Change Theory highlights that sustainable growth doesn't come from dramatic, one-time interventions, but from small, consistent interactions that build belief and energy over time. Everyday moments of hope, compassion, and feedback activate positive emotions that reinforce commitment and resilience (Boyatzis, Smith, & Van Oosten, 2019). Over time, these micro-experiences accumulate into meaningful, lasting change, reminding leaders that culture isn't rebuilt in a single retreat or keynote—it's renewed in the daily rhythm of conversations, check-ins, and acts of recognition.

When the culture feels dull or disconnected, leaders can rekindle it by embracing intentional, emotionally intelligent practices that bring back clarity and connection:

- **Begin by actively bringing teams together** around a shared purpose, whether through recent wins, customer impact stories, or revisiting the "why" behind the work. These moments realign hearts and minds.

- **Use one-on-one check-ins** not only for performance updates but as a space to explore what energizes or drains each team member, helping them reconnect with the mission on a personal level.

- **Focus on micro-moments**—acts of kindness, ingenuity, or collaboration—and celebrate them publicly. These small recognitions help transmit powerful values.

- **Establish structured rituals for renewal**, such as quarterly "culture pulse" huddles, rounds of gratitude at meetings, or regular peer shout-outs. Once these routines are woven into daily life, culture stops being something you chase and becomes something you live.

Most companies don't wake up one day and realize their culture is broken. It happens slowly. Quietly. It begins with a compromise here, a blind eye there. Onboarding gets rushed because "there's no time." A high-performing but toxic employee gets a pass. A manager cuts corners under pressure and is rewarded for the results. Over time, it reinforces the bad behavior. No single moment destroys the system. But collectively, they send a silent message: what you tolerate matters more than what you value. You don't usually lose your culture in a headline-making scandal. You lose it the day the team stops laughing in meetings and nobody notices.

No one understands this better than Johnson & Johnson. During the 1982 Tylenol crisis, when product tampering caused several consumer deaths, the company didn't wait for backlash or weigh the cost of a quiet fix. They recalled thirty-one million bottles from shelves, costing over $100 million. They weren't just reacting to headlines; they were responding to their Credo. Customers first, always. When pressure mounted, those values became the playbook. Their culture wasn't just on paper; it was put into practice. And in the company's toughest moment, it held firm.

Contrast that with Boeing. Once the gold standard of aviation safety and engineering excellence, Boeing's culture shifted under the pressure to compete with Airbus. The drive to cut costs and accelerate production of the 737 MAX sidelined the very engineers who had built Boeing's reputation. Safety gave way to speed. When two tragic crashes claimed 346 lives, the damage was not just financial but cultural: the public's belief in Boeing's name was shaken worldwide. This wasn't simply a product failure; it was a cultural failure, where stated values no longer aligned with daily decisions. Yet in the aftermath, Boeing was forced to confront its drift. Leadership changes, a recommitment to transparency, and reforms in engineering oversight have begun the slow work of rebuilding confidence in this iconic brand. The lesson is sobering but also hopeful: a culture can lose its way under pressure, but with humility, accountability, and a return to its roots, it can still be redeemed.

Leaders who create space for thoughtful reflection and reconnection help their teams reset and rediscover their shared sense of purpose. These kinds of "operating rhythms" have been shown to significantly reduce burnout and increase alignment (Shah, 2019). Simple, consistent moments—whether a quick huddle, a story shared in a meeting, or even a pause to breathe—can become cultural tuning forks. They don't slow the work; they clarify it.

That's exactly what Jonathan Nolen, an engineering leader at LaunchDarkly, discovered. His team implemented an iterative rhythm of stand-ups, retrospectives, and check-ins, not just to organize tasks but to reinforce values. These rituals weren't just procedural; they were cultural. As Nolen put it, they "allowed the company to live its values in the day-to-day," structuring the work in a way that helped people feel the culture, not just hear about it (Nolen, 2021).

You don't have to be the most captivating leader to build an unforgettable culture, but you must show up consistently with care, clarity, and conviction. Day after day. Meeting after meeting. One interaction at a time. Culture isn't a building you finish and admire forever. It's a ship you sail. If you stop steering, even briefly, the currents of distraction, ego, and apathy will take over. Drift happens fast. However, the fix is about being present and recommitting to the values that have brought you to where you are today. It's deciding again, and again, to lead with love, live with intention, and keep choosing your people.

The lesson? When culture shifts, you either identify it early or it catches you later—at ten times the cost. That's why leaders can't just build culture initially; they must also protect it as the business changes, which brings us to the next challenge: how to safeguard that culture when growth and change arrive.

Leading Through Growth and Change

Growth is a beautiful thing, but if you're not paying attention, it can quietly erode the very culture that made that growth possible. Success brings new people, new pressures, and new opportunities. The bigger you get, the more weight your decisions carry. Expansion magnifies everything: the good and the bad. A small misalignment at ten employees might go unnoticed. At one hundred or 1,000? It becomes a gaping hole.

That's why every new chapter, whether it's opening a new location, bringing on a key hire, or navigating a leadership shift, must be anchored back to values. Leaders must tell the stories that shaped who they are, share what's nonnegotiable, model it, then hire and coach it. If protecting culture means slowing down growth, that's not weakness; it's wisdom. One of the best lines I ever heard during a season of rapid expansion was: *"Grow fast enough to chase your dreams, but slow enough to protect your soul."* That stuck with me. Because growth that costs your business its culture isn't really growth, it's just expansion. And expansion without values eventually collapses under its own weight.

Consistency, not intensity, is what preserves culture. Authentic culture isn't built on big moments or grand gestures but in the steady rhythm of leaders showing up with clarity and care. Fear-based cultures might drive short-term results, but they burn people out and drive talent away. Love-based cultures create belonging and resilience. They give people the freedom to fail forward, to speak their minds, and to remain committed to the mission. When people feel loved at work—yes, loved—they fight harder, stay longer, and give more of themselves because they believe in what you are trying to accomplish.

At Dutch Bros, culture is cultivated through rituals such as Dub Shots, mentorships, and servant leadership. New hires don't just *hear* about the values; they *see* them lived in the trenches. A shift leads to stocking shelves when the team is falling behind. A regional manager cleaning up after hours or an executive slinging drinks in the drive-thru because they saw a long line forming. Presence isn't performative; it was modeled. These moments stitched the culture together tighter than any memo ever could.

Few things are as memorable as the "Trav Talks" that happened monthly at Dutch Bros. These motivational presentations by co-founder and former CEO Travis Boersma provided inspiration, enthusiasm and tools to boost the entire brand. What began in 2018 as weekly in-person gatherings at the Grants Pass, OR, headquarters evolved into Zoom broadcasts from Tempe, Arizona, reaching Broistas across the country. And true to Trav's style, these aren't dry corporate updates. One minute, he will be talking about operational excellence, the next cracking a joke that has the whole room laughing, before sharing an emotional story about his brother or the company's grassroots beginnings. That mix of personal encouragement and professional focus reinforces Dutch Bros' "people-first," love-infused culture. Employees often leave not just with new tasks or updates, but with lighter shoulders, a laugh still lingering in the air, and a renewed sense of pride in being part of something bigger, something that matters.

That foundation was tested during the pandemic in 2021. The sudden disconnect necessitated a companywide pivot to completion. With no script to follow, leaders and teams improvised, creating a rhythm of multiple weekly check-ins, newsletters, and constant encouragement. While most employees were encouraged to stay home, communication with vendors, suppliers, and contractors never stopped. Only a handful of people traveled, but everyone was connected. Decisions weren't always popular, but the priority was clear: protect our people and the customers we served. And it worked. That year, in the middle of a global crisis, the team delivered seventy-five new shops, proof that when culture is rooted in values, it can not only endure storms but also emerge stronger.

A crisis shouldn't break a culture; it should expose it. At Dutch Bros, the values are real, and because of that, the company has continued to rise under pressure. What surfaced in those moments was steadiness, candor, and care. Leaders communicated openly and made decisions with transparency, ensuring that people's well-being was protected and their work would continue. The experience proved that resilience isn't about perfection under pressure; it's about showing up with clarity and humanity. Growth and crisis will continue to stretch organizations. Still, when people witness their culture held in difficult times, anchored in values with love as the foundation, it deepens their conviction and strengthens the organization for what comes next.

Building Culture for the Future

Strong culture isn't just about survival; it's about building a future where innovation and belonging thrive. Culture is the soil that allows ideas to grow. World-class organizations prove this time and again.

Take *3M's "15% Rule"*, which gives employees dedicated time to pursue projects outside their formal responsibilities. The result? Breakthroughs like the Post-it Note and numerous other inventions have driven 3M's reputation as a pioneer. The real genius wasn't just in the products; it was in creating a culture where curiosity was rewarded and exploration wasn't seen as a waste of time, but as an investment in growth.[74]

At *Pixar*, improvement is nurtured through its now-famous *Braintrust meetings*, where directors present unfinished work to peers who are free to critique without hierarchy. [75] What makes it powerful isn't the feedback itself, but the environment: respect is nonnegotiable, and candor is safe. This model creates a rhythm of iteration that protects bold storytelling. It shows that when leaders flatten the hierarchy of ideas—even temporarily—they unlock creativity that no single executive could generate alone.

Adobe took a different route with its *Kickbox program*. Instead of just telling employees they had permission to innovate, they handed them a literal red box with a prepaid $1,000

---

[74] Fisher, Lawrence M. "At 3M, Time to Think About Thinking." The New York Times, June 2, 2003.
[75] Isaacson, Walter. "Think Like Pixar: 7 Lessons from the Studio's Creative Culture." Wired, November 17, 2015.

credit card, development tools, and a simple mandate: "Don't break the law but go wild." The message was clear: innovation requires trust.[76] That belief has sparked more than 1,000 projects and reinforced a cultural signal: ideas are worth betting on, and so are the people who create them.

Together, these examples demonstrate that growth doesn't emerge from strategy, but from cultures that provide people with space and the belief that their ideas matter. Research backs it up. Amy Edmondson's work on psychological safety shows that teams that feel safe to speak up consistently outperform those that don't (Edmondson, 2019).[77] PwC found that while 79 percent of leaders view innovation as a driver of growth, less than half believe their culture truly supports it (PwC, 2021).[78]

And it's not just about systems; it's also about perspective. A sweeping analysis of over thirty million scientific papers, conducted by the University of Colorado and Northwestern, found that diverse research teams consistently produced more top-cited, high-impact work than homogenous groups of the same size.[79] Diversity alone doesn't guarantee origination, but paired with a culture that amplifies different voices, it becomes rocket fuel.

That's why the conversation about culture has to move from "how do we protect it now?" to "what kind of legacy are we building next?" This is where leaders must zoom out. Culture

---

[76] Touhill, Dale. "Inside Adobe's Kickbox Toolkit for Innovation." Forbes, July 15, 2015.
[77] Edmondson, Amy C. "The Fearless Organization: Creating Psychological Safety in the Workplace for Learning, Innovation, and Growth." Wiley, 2018.
[78] PwC. "PwC Innovation Benchmark 2023." PwC, 2023.
[79] Wuchty, Stefan, and Brian Uzzi. "Diversity and Creativity in Science and Engineering." PNAS, vol. 112, no. 35, 2015.

isn't just about solving today's fires; it's about designing a workplace that inspires the next generation.

When I think about culture, I think about the kind of company I'd want my kids to join one day, where love fuels performance and people elevate each other higher. That's the legacy worth building. Not just profits or expansion, but places where people thrive, belong, and dare to dream.

If we can build the right culture, the culture will, in turn, help develop others. It shapes you into a leader who listens more deeply, leads with more humility, and dares to believe that business can be a force for good.

That's what it means to steer the soul of your business back home.

When culture finds its way home again, something remarkable happens. The tension eases, creativity returns, and work starts to feel like purpose again. That's the gift of alignment—it doesn't just rebuild organizations; it restores people. Because when a culture is anchored in love and led with clarity, what grows next is joy.

CHAPTER 14

A Culture of Joy

"The best leaders are clear. They continually light the way, and in the process, let each person know that what they do makes a difference."
—Robert Kiefner Greenleaf (American business executive and the founder of the modern servant leadership movement)

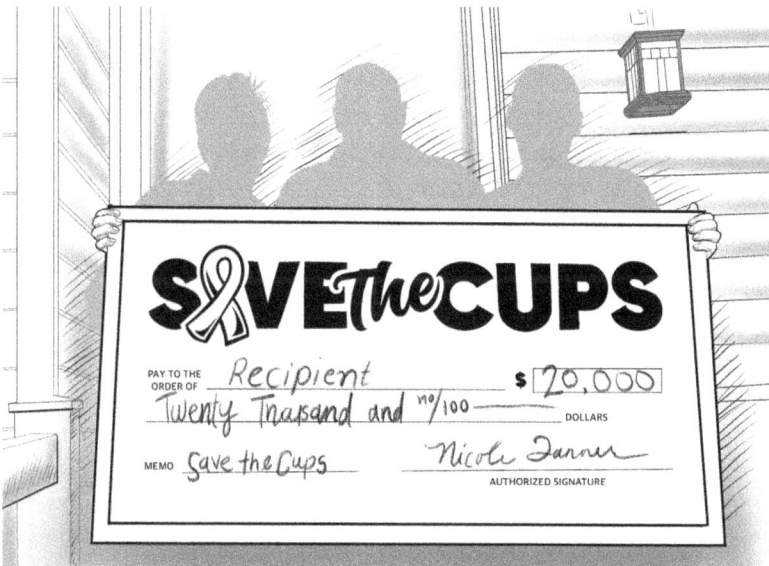

From Survivor to Salvation: The Birth of Save the Cups

In 2009, Swig founder Nicole Robison, a busy mother of five, was diagnosed with an aggressive and rare form of breast cancer. She fought bravely with the support of her friends and family, but without the cushion of health insurance. As she recovered from surgery, Nicole found herself facing over $12,000 in medical expenses, more than she could possibly manage on her own; however, a good friend and local donor stepped in, quietly paying the bills. This left Nicole with a single $100 balance and a full heart.

That one act of kindness changed everything.

The following year (2010), Nicole opened the first Swig location in St. George, Utah, with a simple idea: to create a drive-thru drink stop serving custom sodas and sweet treats. What began as a small-town shop quickly helped pioneer the "dirty soda" craze across the western U.S. As a result, Swig became more than just a business; it evolved into a deeper mission, one that gave Nicole a way to honor the generosity she received by helping others through their own battles.

Eleven years later, in 2020, she launched "Save the Cups," a dedicated campaign during Breast Cancer Awareness Month to raise funds through special drinks, merch, and customer donations. In its first year alone, Swig raised over $161,000, helping to ease medical debt for dozens of women in need.

Since then, Save the Cups has grown into a movement. By October 2024, the campaign had raised over $1 million in just five years, offering real relief to families facing crippling medical bills. To date, Swig has directly helped at least sixty-five families, stepping in at the exact moment they needed support the most.

It's a perfect illustration of the subtle power of giving others credit for their strength and resilience that helps to shape the culture of those around you: customers, employees, and leaders. Nicole's survivor story became a lifeline for others. In honoring the generosity shown to her, she didn't hide from her scars or her success. She used both to encourage others, choosing to pass the spotlight to those still in the fight. And in doing so, she didn't just build a campaign; she also created a movement. She built a culture of generosity that now defines the heart of Swig.

Nicole often says, "Swig was born, so it could lead us to Save the Cups." Hers is a story of turning pain into purpose, not by holding onto the spotlight, but by stepping back and lifting others into it. This isn't just charity; it's a living legacy of a single act of grace, and a reminder that authentic leadership begins when we give others more credit than we take for ourselves.

Culture That Echoes Beyond the Walls

Here's the truth most leaders miss: culture doesn't stop at the front door. Done right, it radiates outward, touching customers, vendors, neighbors, and entire communities. Strong culture is contagious. It seeps into every interaction, every community event, and every ripple your business makes beyond its own four walls. When built with intention, love, and bold authenticity, it becomes more than a business; it becomes a movement.

From day one, Dutch Bros decided to focus on people first. The mission wasn't about caffeine, but connection. Customers weren't just served; they were seen, remembered, and told they were loved. That love extended far beyond the drive-thru. Fundraisers like *Drink One for Dane* and *Buck for Kids* have raised millions for ALS research and local youth organizations. These aren't marketing campaigns, but rather the natural byproduct of a culture that prioritizes people above all else.

Other brands prove the same point in different ways. Patagonia built its reputation by putting the planet before profit. When founder Yvon Chouinard transferred ownership of the company to a trust to fight climate change, it was culture in action. Patagonia doesn't just sell jackets; they invite customers into a movement to protect the world in which those jackets are worn.

Whether it's Dutch Bros inviting customers into love or Patagonia rallying people around the environment, both show that when values are lived, they ripple beyond the balance sheet. Throughout this book, several companies effectively embody their culture. But this book isn't just about companies. It's about people. It's about you. The test of leadership is not whether you can build something profitable; it's whether you can create something that lasts.

Culture is how you treat people inside the building. Branding is how the world experiences that treatment outside. The best branding doesn't shout but echoes your culture. It amplifies what's already real. When your team embodies values like kindness, excellence, and grit, your brand doesn't have to try so hard to look good. The world will see it, feel it, and embrace it. Branding is the soul of your culture made visible.

But be warned: if you claim to care about the planet but your actions contradict this, people will notice. Your brand isn't defined by what you say; it's about what people say about you. If you preach community but treat customers like numbers, they'll walk away. If you claim to value your team but underpay and overlook them, the breakdown will eventually surface. In today's connected world, and especially under the scrutiny of social media, authenticity is no longer optional; it's the whole game. Live your culture first, then tell the story. That's the only order that works.

People fall in love with brands that feel alive, warm, real, and human. So, talk like a person. Laugh a little. Show some weirdness. Be a little messy if it means being more real. Your imperfections are part of your power—they make you relatable and more believable. That's why this chapter isn't about marketing but ensuring that the soul of your business—the love, the leadership, the humanity you've built on the inside—flows just as strongly outside.

Before you shout your culture from the rooftops, take a minute to check the mirror. If there's a gap between what you say and what you live, don't panic. Just start closing it. When your internal culture is strong and your external brand is honest, something beautiful happens. You stop selling. You start belonging. You don't just build a customer base. You build a community. A community that shows up for you. That forgives you when you make a mistake. That becomes your loudest, proudest storytellers.

Here are five simple ways to let your culture echo beyond your walls:

1. **Get involved locally.** Sponsor a Little League team. Join the Chamber of Commerce. Host a neighborhood clean-up.

2. **Empower your employees to give.** Offer time off to volunteer. Match donations. Let them choose causes that matter to them.

3. **Make your space feel human.** Add plants, music, artwork, and stories. Create a lasting impression that stays in people's minds.

4. **Talk to your customers.** Really talk. Learn names. Remember orders. Ask about their lives—and mean it.

5. **Lead with love.** Be generous. Be kind. And do it again tomorrow.

These are strategic, culture-building decisions that deepen your company's roots in the community. But the objective measure of culture isn't just in what you do today, it's in what outlasts you.

Why Everett?

Culture doesn't just exist in boardrooms or brand campaigns. It reveals itself in the quiet moments when no one is watching. Sometimes it's a small act of kindness that shifts the course of someone's life. I'll never forget this story shared by Teal Dennis, a regional activation coach from the Dutch Bros family. Here is her story:

It was December 2016, and I was in Everett, Washington, just days away from opening my first Dutch Bros shop. The crew was inside—six mobsters and my lead, Kate Lonstrom. We had been working into the evening, prepping for the launch, running drills, stocking, and training the new team. It was already dark outside, and the mix of nerves and excitement filled the stand. As the night moved on, I caught a glimpse of someone approaching the building. Soon, a man was standing in front of the drive-thru window.

Right away, Kate leaned in beside me, just to make sure I felt safe. The man looked a little beat up, clearly going through something. Kate noticed too. She offered to take it, but I said, "Nah, I got it."

Hesitantly, I opened the window just wide enough to let the man in. "Hi. How's it going?"

He replied, "Not really that good."

The man looked a little rough around the edges, a little worn, like life had taken a toll. He told us he had just been released from jail: no place to stay, no money, and nowhere to go. But we continued talking, and I let him know that we were "opening tomorrow" and offered him a drink. 'Nothing fancy—just something warm,' he requested. The trainees moved quietly behind us as Kate and I stood at the window with the man.

He continued talking, sharing more about his circumstances and how life had led him to this point. At one point, he pulled out a folded certificate from his backpack. He was trying to get his dog back from the pound, and he didn't want to do that until he got his life in order. "Will you hold onto this certificate for me? It's the form I need to get my dog released." He said he didn't want to mess it up while he was out on the street.

I remember thinking, **"Is he ever going to come back? Will we ever see him again?"**

Kate and I found a place in the filing cabinet in the back office and tucked the certificate in a safe place. Before he left, we went out to hug him and wished him well. And then he was gone.

After opening the shop, we had forgotten about the encounter, and things were just starting to get settled in. Several weeks later, a car pulled up, and a man in the back seat rolled down the window and asked for Kate and me by name. We both walked over, thinking it was someone we knew from work. The man said, "Do you remember me?"

Kate and I looked at each other. We didn't, not at first.

Then he said, "It's Caleb. I came by a few weeks ago. You have my dog certificate."

Then he paused and looked at us, and I'll never forget what he said next.

"That night, I didn't tell you. . .But I was planning to take my life. I had a plan. I didn't think anyone cared. But you did. You talked to me without judging me. You just listened. And the embrace you gave me changed everything."

He told us that he was now living with friends. Had just started a construction job, and life was getting back on track. Most importantly, he and his friends were on their way to pick up his dog.

Kate and I just stood there. Speechless. Emotional. Grateful.

People asked me all the time, "Why would Dutch Bros open a shop in Everett?" That location on Broadway had a reputation. High drug activity. Rough neighborhood. People would often ask, "Why there?"

And my answer was always the same: Because they need us. Because we belong there. Because we can make a difference.

That's who Dutch Bros is. Showing up in the places people don't expect love to live—and reminding them it still does.

That night could've gone so differently. But what made the difference was an opportunity to pause—a moment of kindness, with a bit of love, that allowed for a deep human connection. From what we hear, Caleb is still doing well today, and we are grateful to have been a part of this moment in his life.

That story still moves me. It reminds us that culture isn't about where we build, it's about *why* we show up. Love belongs everywhere. And sometimes, the most powerful leadership moment arrives at a drive-thru window.

What Is Your Legacy?

Over these pages, we've walked through stories of growth, loss, grit, and grace. We've looked at culture in coffee shops, construction sites, and boardrooms. We've discussed consistency over intensity, love over fear, and service over ego. All of it comes down to one truth: leadership is not about being in charge; it's about taking care of those in your charge.

If you've made it to Chapter 14, I already know something important about you: YOU CARE. You care about doing things the right way. You care about people. You care about what this thing you're building means, not just what it makes. And that's the good news—you're already on the right path. Now just keep walking it. Keep leading with joy. With purpose. And with the kind of love that multiplies as it moves.

In *"Ego Is the Enemy,"* Ryan Holiday presents a compelling case that unchecked ego, self-importance, and the craving for recognition are the silent saboteurs of both personal growth and organizational integrity. [80] He draws from historical and modern leadership to show how true greatness is often born not from bravado, but from restraint, humility, and discipline, and how the best leaders let purpose, not pride, set the pace. When values genuinely lead, they extend outward, shaping how teams treat one another, how companies respond in crisis, and how leaders carry themselves. Holiday's message is deeply affirming: the most significant transformations, both personal and organizational, come from those who commit to something bigger than themselves.

At this stage in my life, I wear the title "elder" with pride *(most days)*, mainly because I've earned every laugh line and gray hair along the way. But being an elder comes with a duty: to set the next generation up for success, not just with opportunity, but with wisdom. That means teaching them more than how to punch a clock or run a store. It means showing them how to be good businesspeople, responsible community members, and rock-solid leaders.

---

[80] Holiday, Ryan. Ego Is the Enemy. Portfolio, 2016.

That last one matters most: leadership. When someone walks through your doors, they don't just bring a résumé; they bring their whole life with them. If someone comes from a fractured home, you'll often see the weight of that show up in how they work, communicate, and handle stress. That's why we must teach young people how to show up, take responsibility, and care for one another. When you build character first, competence follows, and leadership begins.

Some of our younger team members may not have attended college, and that's okay. At Dutch Bros, the focus was on compelling futures, building Broistas up to run stores, lead teams, and grow into leaders with knowledge and discernment. And guess what—they are making more money than they ever imagined. These people skipped the classroom and still earned their Ph.D. with grit, hustle, and heart. College isn't the only ticket to success. Sometimes, work is the education.

And in the workplace, cultural values matter. I've worked with franchisees from diverse backgrounds, and I've seen firsthand what happens when individuals bring their traditions, work ethic, and family pride into the business. Immigrant communities, including those from South America, the Middle East, Asia, and others, often embody the exact traits that fuel success: discipline, humility, and a deep respect for family and education. These aren't just admirable; they're advantageous.

Ultimately, culture is the one thing that no competitor can replicate. Products can be duplicated. Processes can be reverse-engineered. But how you make people feel is yours alone.

Robert K. Greenleaf, the father of servant leadership, reminded us that "the servant-leader is servant first." That principle reshaped how I have thought about influence, not as a tool for control, but as an opportunity for humility. The best leaders don't climb above their teams; they lift from below. They listen more than they speak, support more than they shine, and seek to understand first. If legacy is measured not by the titles held but by the lives touched, then the most significant legacy a leader can leave is a culture where people are inspired to serve others.

That's the legacy worth chasing. Not applause, not titles, not the fleeting glow of quarterly success, but a culture that breathes life into people and outlives you. Because when you get culture right, it doesn't just build a business; it builds a culture. It builds people. And those people carry it forward, multiplying the good long after you're gone.

This book is called *No EGO Policy* for a reason. Ego builds empires that collapse. Love builds cultures that endure. And now, it's your turn to lead with love, to choose service over self, and to build something that lasts.

Lead Without **EGO, Love** Without **Limits, and Create** Something **Unforgettable.**

CHAPTER 15

The Culture Checklist

"Culture isn't created in a single moment—it's maintained in a million tiny ones."

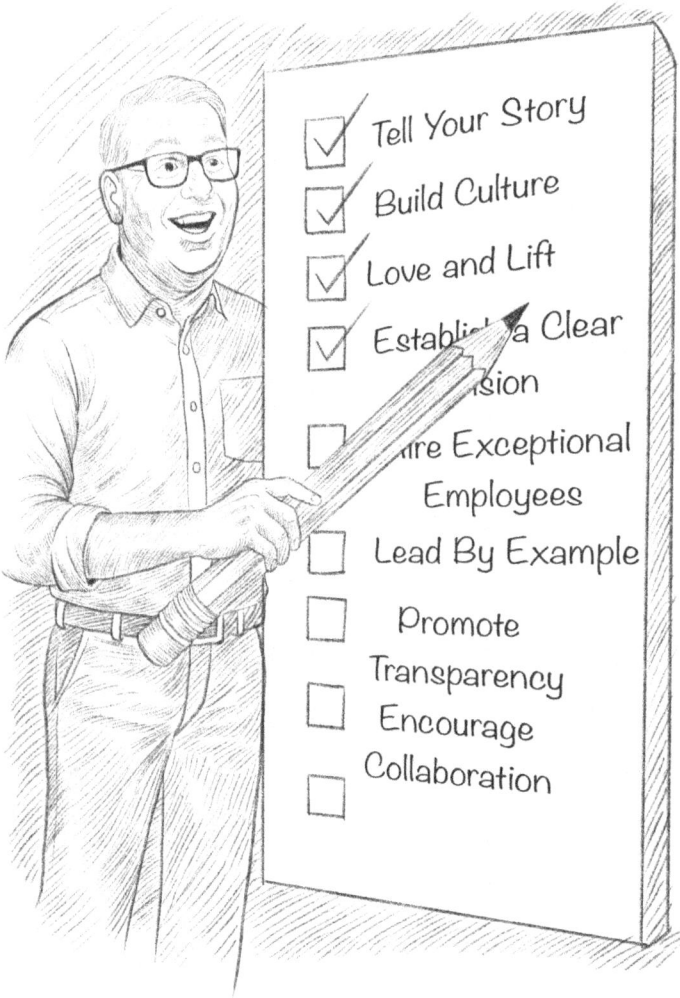

How to Begin

Building a culture isn't a one-time event; it's a journey, and like any meaningful expedition, it needs a map. This chapter is your compass. It distills every lesson from the past fourteen chapters into a practical, step-by-step guide to building, sustaining, and protecting the kind of culture that not only performs but lasts. Think of it as your gardener's guide. You've planted something beautiful. Now let's make sure it keeps blooming.

Section 1: Start with the Story

Every culture begins with a story—but not just any story. It must be real. It must be rooted in truth. And it must connect. If the story isn't being told, the culture will write its own version—and often, it won't align with your vision.

Key Concepts:
Before you talk about values or policies, ask yourself:

☐ Is your origin story clearly known and shared with the team?
☐ Is your purpose (your why) evident in your operations and values?
☐ Is your story authentic and emotionally resonant?

Section 2: Build the Foundation

Culture can't be layered on later; it must be poured into the foundation. This means leadership must model what matters. Values should be lived, not just read about. And those values must be clear, fair, and consistently reinforced with kindness and accountability. "Fair, Firm, and Friendly" isn't a slogan—it's a survival strategy.

Key Concepts:
☐ Are your company values actively modeled by leadership?
☐ Do you reinforce values through daily behaviors and decisions?
☐ Is your team clear on what behavior is expected and rewarded?

Section 3: Hire to Protect the House

Culture is only as strong as your people. Don't just hire for skill—hire for fit. Better yet, hire for *add*. Onboarding should be more than just training; it should be a cultural immersion experience. Protect your house from the start by making sure every new person knows what you stand for and why it matters. Culture grows stronger when everyone sees themselves in it. Ensure your table has sufficient seating.

Key Concepts:
☐ Do your hiring practices screen for both values and performance?
☐ Is onboarding used to immerse new hires in your culture?
☐ Are employees taught how to protect the culture from day one?

Section 4: Lead with Love, Not Ego

EGO means Edging God Out—and it edges people out, too. Real leadership demands heart, humility, and hard conversations. Love doesn't mean avoiding accountability; it means delivering it with empathy. A great leader listens, encourages, and corrects with care and consideration. That's how trust is built.

Key Concepts:
☐ Do your leaders coach with empathy and clarity?
☐ Are hard conversations held with compassion and consistency?
☐ Is ego-free leadership modeled at all levels?

Section 5: Grow Your People

Development isn't a perk—it's a cultural expectation. Recognize effort. Create room for stretch assignments. Coach people up, not out. When you grow leaders from within, you don't just create bench strength—you create belief. And belief fuels retention and performance.

Key Concepts:
☐ Do you regularly recognize and reward great work?
☐ Are employees offered meaningful development opportunities?
☐ Is leadership potential cultivated from within the team?

Section 6: Maintain the Flame

Culture can't survive on past momentum. Protect it daily. Celebrate small wins. Check your emotional pulse. Create rituals that reinforce identity and energize the team. This is how you avoid burnout while keeping the fire lit.

Key Concepts:
☐ Do you celebrate small wins and progress regularly?
☐ Are rituals in place that reinforce identity and connection?
☐ Is emotional well-being monitored and supported by leadership?

Culture Pulse Check
☐ Do people smile when they come in?
☐ Are employees referring friends to work here?
☐ Is feedback shared regularly and respectfully?
☐ Are new ideas welcomed–or shot down?
☐ Are people growing, or just coasting?

Rituals That Matter
☐ Weekly shoutouts
☐ Start meetings with gratitude
☐ Culture check-ins
☐ Open calendar hours
☐ Community service days

Section 7: Guard the House

Consistency is the secret sauce of culture. Great culture doesn't happen occasionally–it happens *every day*. Revisit your values often. Reward behaviors that reflect those values. And never ask for something you aren't willing to model. When leadership walks the walk, culture thrives.

Key Concepts:
☐ Are values reinforced through rewards and consequences?
☐ Are behaviors consistent across teams and leadership?
☐ Do leaders hold themselves accountable to the same standards?

Silent Killers of Culture

- Gossip
- Burnout
- Favoritism
- Mission drift
- Stagnant leadership

Section 8: Rebuild When It Slips

Every culture drifts. The test measures how quickly and honestly you respond. Don't hide the issues—name them. Own the missteps. Involve the team in rebuilding. Return to the *why*. Recommit to the values. This is how you restore what matters.

Key Concepts:
☐ Do you have a way to detect when culture is slipping?
☐ Are missteps named and addressed openly?
☐ Have you created space for the team to recommit and rebuild?

Section 9: Let It Radiate

Culture doesn't end inside the building—it echoes into your brand. Customers can feel if what you preach is real. Ensure that your external presence aligns with your internal values. Lead with authenticity. Serve with heart. That's how culture becomes a legacy.

Key Concepts:
☐ Does your external image match your internal culture?
☐ Are you telling a consistent and honest story across channels?
☐ Do customers and partners feel your values through interaction?

The Leadership Mirror: Monthly Reflection

☐ Am I living the values I expect others to live?
☐ Do my team members feel safe bringing feedback to me?
☐ Have I celebrated someone's growth or success this week?

☐ Am I walking through the trenches with my people or watching from above?
☐ When things go wrong, do I blame or do I build?

The Final 10 Questions – Your Culture Compass

1. What do we actually believe in?
2. What behavior do we reward—and what do we tolerate?
3. How do we onboard new people into this culture?
4. Do our systems match our values?
5. How do we handle mistakes?
6. Who feels heard? Who doesn't?
7. When was the last time we laughed together?
8. How do we grow our people?
9. Would I want my kid to work here?
10. Are we building something worth remembering?

Final Thought: Culture Is Kingdom Work

I'd be remiss if I didn't leave you with something bigger than checklists and playbooks. Building culture, when done with love, integrity, and service, reflects the highest calling we have: to love others as God first loved us.

- Hire and fire by values, not by convenience.
- Model the culture you preach.
- Tell the stories that make people believe.
- Create rituals that celebrate love in action.
- Communicate with honesty and humility.
- Embed your values in every system.
- Listen with ears tuned for the heart.

Most importantly, lead with servant leadership at your core.

Elevate others higher than yourself.

Leave every space better than you found it.

Culture isn't a one-time build. It's a living system. Check this list quarterly. Adapt as you grow. Share wins. Own missteps. And above all—lead with love, not EGO.

Because when you get culture right, you're not just running a business.

You're building a little piece of heaven here on Earth.

And friend, there's no greater return on investment than that.

Build with love, and it will grow beyond your reach—but never beyond your purpose.

A Letter to the Builders of Tomorrow

*The future belongs to the people who build
with love and lead with heart.*

Dear Builder,

If you've made it this far, it's because something in you still believes that leadership can be different, that culture can be human, and that business can still have heart. You're right. And you're exactly the kind of leader the world needs.

This book has always been a letter to those who build with love, who know that, deep down, business can be beautiful. It's for the dreamers and doers who still believe that people matter more than process, and for those who think culture is the foundation to building a legacy for the world of tomorrow.

I didn't always feel confident in that belief. I've stumbled upon plenty of opportunities to share my belief about the importance of a strong culture, but I've missed them many times. I have failed both publicly and privately, and I have had days when I questioned whether I was suited for a business environment. But the truth that's carried me through it all is simple: when you lead with love, the rest finds its way.

Someone's watching you right now, hoping to learn what leadership looks like. It might be a teammate, a peer, or a child in the backseat listening to how you handle a hard day. They're watching how you show up, how you treat people, how you speak when the pressure is on or how you lead when no one's clapping. You're shaping what leadership feels like for someone else, mentoring them—directly or indirectly—through your actions, simply by showing up.

I was only able to succeed because others reached back to pull me forward, mentors, friends, and family who believed in me long before I believed in myself. Their encouragement changed my life. Now, it's my turn. And it's yours too. Because legacy isn't what we build, it's who we build. We do it alone or as a group. But we must do it.

There will be hard days. Keep going anyway. Find your people. Be someone else's person. Return to your *why* when the noise gets loud. Because this isn't just business, it's a purpose.

Thank you for joining me on this journey. May you continue to build things that last, love people deeply, and lead in a way that reminds others what true humanity in business looks like.

With gratitude,
Daniel

The Culture We Leave Behind

Somewhere out there, someone is walking into their first day on the job.

They've got a mix of nerves and excitement in their stomach. They're wondering what kind of people they'll meet, if they'll be accepted, and whether this new job is another stop along their path to finding a place where they finally feel like they belong.

And that's where you come in.

If you have journeyed with me to this book's close, a light now burns within you. A spark. A conviction that culture isn't merely words that hang on the wall, it's woven into the fabric of how we lead. The mantle now rests in your hands, and with it, the power to ignite the next generation of leaders.

It will be how you make people feel, how you carry yourself, what you protect, what you prioritize, and what you pour into others.

We don't always get to see the result of the seeds we plant. But that's not why we grow them. We do it because we believe that something better is possible. That people are worth investing in. That work can be meaningful. That leadership—done with love—can actually change the world.

So plant the seeds. Tell the stories. Lift people up. Be kind. And keep building cultures that matter.

The world needs what you're building.

Keep going.

Acknowledgments

The legacy of leadership lives not in power or profit, but in service to others. When leaders serve with their hearts, culture grows roots that hold fast, bear fruit, and endure across generations.

We've all heard the saying, "It takes a village." This book is a testament to that truth. To the many leaders, peers, family members, friends, and even those who didn't feel compelled to bless my career along the way, you each played a role in shaping the best parts of me.

To my immediate family, thank you for the roots. You gave me the foundation to grow, to stumble, and to rise again. You taught me that love starts at home and that real success is measured in hugs, laughter, and the grace we give each other daily. Your support, prayers, and presence have been the quiet strength beneath everything I've ever built. Family is where love lives, not just in biology, but in the bonds that bind us together. You've taught me that family is about shared love, shared faith, and shared purpose.

To my mother and father: God used your lives, your love, and even your pain to shape the person I am today.

Dad, your loss was a wound I never expected. But I carry only the memory of a father at his best. You were a devoted husband to our mother, a man who loved fiercely, disciplined with conviction, and would walk through fire to protect his children. Your belief in people was often tested, but your passion could move mountains.

Although in one tragic moment, darkness seemed to have won, it was only for a moment. Because in the ashes of that moment, God met me. He used your absence to call me deeper into compassion, humility, and purpose. And through it all, I've come to believe that no story is beyond redemption, not even ours.

Mom, you are a living testimony of God's grace. At ninety-one years old, you've endured deep loss with unwavering faith and shown me what it means to walk with God even when the path seems broken. In your quiet strength is a reminder that light still shines through cracked vessels, and that the Holy Spirit heals what human hands cannot. When the night is long, you've taught me to cling to the promise that "weeping may endure for a night, but joy comes in the morning" (*Psalm 30:5*). Your resilience is proof that faith doesn't just survive the storm, it sings through it.

To my brothers, who walked through the same loss but carried it in ways I may never fully understand, your quiet strength and presence have always meant more to me than words could express. Your intelligence, talent, and heart constantly inspire me. You are a gift, and there is nothing stronger than the Batty Bros. I'm proud to be called your brother, and I love you both more than you know.

To those I've had the privilege to call "family." The people I've worked beside over the years, the sons and daughters I didn't raise from birth, but who still call me 'Dad' anyway: thank you for the honor and respect. Know this, you are no less mine. Thank you for trusting me, challenging me, and inviting me to your table. Some families are born. Others are built. I'm blessed to have both.

To my team at Dutch Bros, you helped shape this story in more ways than these pages will ever do justice. The love, energy, and commitment you bring every day are culture in motion. I've learned more from working alongside you than I ever did in any classroom, boardroom, or book. This chapter of my life was unforgettable. Thank you for welcoming me into your world and allowing me to share these moments with you.

Tony Sisca, thank you for your kindness and belief in me when I was a teenager and lacked the confidence to believe in myself—you set me on the road toward discovery.

Richard Hunsaker, my mentor and friend, who challenged me, inspired me, and provided me with space to grow. You were the first leader in the workplace who set the tone for what I've sought my entire career. Your integrity, consistency, and belief in people became the standard by which I measure leadership. Thank you for showing me what it means to lead well. Your impact echoes through every page of this book.

Travis Boersma, thank you for giving me the platform to stumble forward, grow, and discover purpose alongside your incredible team of leaders. Christine Schmidt, Brian Maxwell, Joth Ricci, and so many others, your grace, belief in people, and unwavering optimism propelled your teams to greatness. I was simply blessed to be carried by the overflow of your hearts.

To every reader, thank you for letting me into your world. I hope this book makes you smile, think, and feel seen. You're part of this culture too, and now a part of my journey. I'm grateful to share my story, but feel blessed that you were compelled to read it.

This book was an opportunity for me to pay tribute to the people, businesses, and others who have played pivotal roles in my life. But mostly, the book is for you, the readers.

About the Author

Daniel J. Batty is a developer and culture-driven leader whose career bridges construction, creativity, and compassion. He is the author of *No EGO Policy: Culture Reimagined - Leading with Love & Authenticity*, a transformative guide to leadership that blends real-world business lessons with the timeless power of empathy and purpose to create a culture of success.

A lifelong builder at heart, Daniel's journey began on job sites alongside his father, where he learned that integrity and hard work are the true foundations of success. That early influence shaped a career spanning more than two decades across design, construction, and operations leadership. He has held executive roles with some of the nation's most recognizable brands, including McDonald's, Carl's Jr./Hardee's, Dunkin', and Dutch Bros Coffee—where his leadership helped scale development across fast-growth corporate and franchise systems.

In tandem with his business accomplishments, Daniel has long invested in community, storytelling, and authorship. In January 1999, he received a **Resolution for Outstanding Community Service** from the California State Legislature and a **Recognition of Community Leadership Activities** from the County of Orange. Earlier, from 1998-99, he served as **Contributing Editor** for *Even Par Magazine*, and from 1997-2006, he was a **Contributing Writer** for the *San Clemente Journal*. In 1996, he acted as **Technical Advisor** for the educational video *Recycling Made Easy*, and his bylines have appeared in local publications such as the *Capistrano Valley News*, under the column *Let's Talk Trash*. He was also a **Contributing Author** for *The Question Book* (Bobb Biehl, Thomas Nelson Publishers, 1993) and, most recently, contributed to *The Author's Playbook* by Ray Brehm (2024), available on Amazon and Goodreads.

Daniel's leadership philosophy—rooted in his "No EGO Policy" and "Fair, Firm & Friendly" mantras—emphasizes that culture is not a department, but a daily decision. His writing reflects this belief, drawing from personal experience, faith, and lessons of both triumph and tragedy. The story of his father's passing, a deeply formative event, anchors his message that love and authenticity are the most enduring leadership tools.

Outside the boardroom, Daniel is a dedicated storyteller and community advocate. He supports organizations such as **Surfers Healing**, a nonprofit surf-therapy initiative for children with autism, and he currently has additional books in development.

A native of Southern California, Daniel travels frequently and spends time across the western United States, yet San Clemente, California, will always be home—where he still catches waves whenever he can. When he's not writing or building, you'll find him mentoring emerging leaders, exploring land-development projects, or simply enjoying time with family.

To learn more about Daniel's work, upcoming books, or speaking engagements, visit noegopolicy.com or connect with him on LinkedIn.

Bibliography

Aksu, Halil, ed. "Zappos' Culture of Delivering Happiness: Putting Employees First for Exceptional Customer Service." Digitopia. October 3, 2024. https://digitopia.co/blog/zappos-culture

Amabile, Teresa, Colin Fisher, and Julianna Pillemer. "IDEO's Culture of Helping." *Harvard Business Review*, January–February 2014. https://hbr.org/2014/01/ideos-culture-of-helping

Anand, Nupur. "How Charlie Scharf Got Wells Fargo Out of the Penalty Box." *Reuters*, June 4, 2025. https://www.reuters.com/sustainability/boards-policy-regulation/how-charlie-scharf-got-wells-fargo-out-penalty-box-2025-06-03/

Ayin, Alex. 2025. "How Southwest Airlines Built a High-Performance Culture." ELITE TEAM TACTICS. https://www.eliteteamtactics.com/p/how-southwest-airlines-built-a-high-performance-culture-1dbe

Bellet, Clement, Jan-Emmanuel De Neve, and George Ward. 2023. "Does Employee Happiness Have an Impact on Productivity?" *Management Science* 70 (3), 1656–1679. https://doi.org/10.1287/mnsc.2023.4766

Bock, Laszlo. 2015. *Work Rules!: Insights from Inside Google That Will Transform How You Live and Lead*. Grand Central Pub.

Bolade-Ogunfodun, Yemisi, Matthew Sinnicks, Kleio Akrivou, and Germán Scalzo. 2022. "Exploring the Vulnerability of Practice-Like Activities: An Ethnographic Perspective." *Frontiers in Sociology* 7. https://doi.org/10.3389/fsoc.2022.1003741

Bondarenko, Peter. 2025. "Enron Scandal." In *Encyclopædia Britannica*. https://www.britannica.com/event/Enron-scandal

Boyatzis, Richard E. 2024. *The Science of Change*. Oxford University Press.

Brown, Lisa. "Southwest Airlines' Organizational Culture & Its Characteristics." Panmore Institute. May 14, 2019. https://panmore.com/southwest-airlines-co-organizational-culture-characteristics-analysis

Cameron, Christopher. "Working from Home Can Be Dangerous to Your Health and Stifle Innovation: Study." *New York Post*, August 24, 2024. https://nypost.com/2024/08/24/opinion/working-from-home-can-be-dangerous-to-your-health-and-stifle-innovation-study/

"Careers at Patagonia | Patagonia Jobs." 2024. Patagonia. https://careers.patagonia.com/us/en/

Chick-fil-A. 2025. "Culture & Values." Chick-fil-A. https://www.chick-fil-a.com/careers/culture

Chick-fil-A. 2025. "What Are Chick-Fil-A's Core Values?" Chick-fil-A. https://www.chick-fil-a.com/customer-support/who-we-are/our-culture-and-values/what-are-chick-fil-a-core-values

Chouinard, Yvon. "Earth Is Now Our Only Shareholder." Patagonia. September 14, 2022. https://www.patagonia.com/ownership/

Clance, Pauline Rose and Suzanne Ament Imes. 1978. "The Impostor Phenomenon in High Achieving Women: Dynamics and Therapeutic Intervention." *Psychotherapy: Theory, Research & Practice* 15 (3), 241–247. https://doi.org/10.1037/h0086006

Coulombe, Joe. 2021. *Becoming Trader Joe*. HarperCollins Leadership.

"Culture by the Numbers: The ROI of Workplace Culture Investments." Enculture. June 11, 2025. https://www.enculture. ai/blog/culture-by-the-numbers-the-roi-of-workplace-culture-investments

Dela Rosa, Christine. 2021. "Work Check." Podcast. Atlassian. https://www.atlassian.com/blog/podcast/work-check/season/season-1/do-operating-rhythms-drive-company-culture

Deliso, Meredith. "Theranos Founder Elizabeth Holmes' Conviction Upheld by US Appeals Court." *ABC News*, February 24, 2025. https://abcnews.go.com/Business/theranos-founder-eli zabeth-holmes-conviction-upheld-us-appeals/story?id= 119135714

Delk, Brian. "Imposter Syndrome Reported by 71% of CEOs." *Bloomberg*, June 25, 2024. https://www.bloomberg.com/news/ newsletters/2024-06-25/imposter-syndrome-reported-by-71-of-ceos

Deloitte. 2025. "2025 Global Human Capital Trends." Deloitte Insights. https://www2.deloitte.com/us/en/insights/focus/hu man-capital-trends.html

Diaz, Ana Maria, Marie Boltz, Bart Cockx, and Luz Magdalena Salas. "How Does Working-Time Flexibility Affect Workers' Produc tivity in a Routine Job? Evidence from a Field Experiment." (1). Harvard Dataverse. October 6, 2022. https://doi.org/10.7910/ DVN/AZJOMW

Edmonds, S. Chris. "3 Takeaways from In-N-Out Burger's Work Culture." SmartBrief. March 26, 2024. https://www.smartbrief. com/original/3-takeaways-from-in-n-out-burgers-work-culture

Edmondson, Amy C. 2019. *The Fearless Organization: Creating Psychological Safety in the Workplace for Learning, Innovation, and Growth*. Hoboken, New Jersey: Wiley.

Emmer, Marc. "How Trader Joe's Built an Iconic Brand Through Employee Engagement." Inc.com. January 13, 2020. https://www.inc.com/marc-emmer/how-trader-joes-built-an-iconic-brand-through-employee-engagement.html

"Employment." 2021. In-n-Out.com. https://www.in-n-out.com/employment

EQS Editorial Team. "Elizabeth Holmes & the Theranos Case: History of a Fraud Scandal." EQS Integrity Line. November 22, 2023. https://www.integrityline.com/expertise/blog/elizabeth-holmes-theranos/

Erb, Marcus. "Treating Employees Well Led to Higher Stock Prices During the Pandemic." Great Place to Work®. August 5, 2021. https://www.greatplacetowork.com/resources/blog/treating-employees-well-led-to-higher-stock-prices-during-the-pandemic

"Explore Salesforce Culture and Values." n.d. Trailhead. https://trailhead.salesforce.com/content/learn/modules/salesforce-culture-and-values/explore-salesforce-culture-and-values

FBI. 2016. "Enron." Federal Bureau of Investigation. https://www.fbi.gov/history/famous-cases/enron

Ferguson, Stephanie and Makinizi Hoover. "Understanding America's Labor Shortage: The Most Impacted Industries." U.S. Chamber of Commerce. November 21, 2023. https://www.uschamber.com/workforce/understanding-americas-labor-shortage-the-most-impacted-industries

Franklin-Wallis, Oliver. "Think Like Pixar: 7 Lessons from the Studio's Creative Culture." *Wired*, November 17, 2015. https://www.wired.com/story/pixar-lessons-film-studio-creative-business/

Gainsford, Matt. "Zappos: A Case Study Into Company Culture | Titus Talent Strategies." Titus Talent Strategies.

https://www.titustalent.com/insights/zappos-a-case-study-into-company-culture/

Gallup. 2025. "State of the Global Workplace 2022 Report." Gallup. https://www.gallup.com/workplace/349484/state-of-the-global-workplace.aspx

Garvin, David A. "How Google Sold Its Engineers on Management." *Harvard Business Review*, 91 (12), 74–82. December 2013. https://hbr.org/2013/12/how-google-sold-its-engineers-on-management

Gass, Zach. "Disney's 'Hug Rule' Completely Changes Character Experience." Inside the Magic. January 18, 2024. https://insidethemagic.net/2024/01/hug-rule-completely-changes-character-experience-at-disney-parks-zg1/

Gauthier, Arthur and Joel Bothello. "What Happens When a Company (Like Patagonia) Transfers Ownership to a Nonprofit?" *Harvard Business Review*, October 10, 2022. https://hbr.org/2022/10/what-happens-when-a-company-like-patagonia-becomes-a-nonprofit

"Google Re:Work - Guides: Give Feedback to Managers." 2025. Rework. https://rework.withgoogle.com/intl/en/guides/managers-give-feedback-to-managers

Gulati, Ranjay. "Netflix: A Creative Approach to Culture and Agility - Case No. 56185 - Faculty & Research." Harvard Business School. September 2019. https://www.hbs.edu/faculty/Pages/item.aspx?num=56185

H-E-B. 2022. "H-E-B Corporate Responsibility Report." (Document not publicly available.)

Hackman, J. Richard and Greg R. Oldham. 1980. *Work Redesign*. Reading, MA: Addison-Wesley.

Hall, Cheryl. "Why In-N-Out Burger Is One of America's Best Employers." *Dallas Morning News*, March 1, 2018. https://www.dallasnews.com/business/retail/2018/03/01/why-in-n-out-burger-is-one-of-america-s-best-employers/

Hersey, Paul and Kenneth H. Blanchard. 1969. "Life Cycle Theory of Leadership." *Training and Development Journal* 23 (5), 26-34. https://psycnet.apa.org/record/1970-19661-001?ref=exo-insight

Hill, Linda A., Tarun Khanna, and Emily Stecker. "HCL Technologies (A) - Case No. 9-408-004 - Faculty & Research." Harvard Business School. July 2008. https://www.hbs.edu/faculty/Pages/item.aspx?num=34784

History.com Editors. "Enron Files for Bankruptcy | December 2, 2001 | HISTORY." HISTORY. November 24, 2009. https://www.history.com/this-day-in-history/december-2/enron-files-for-bankruptcy

Holiday, Ryan. 2016. *Ego Is the Enemy*. Profile Books.

Hwang, Chan Young, Seung-Wan Kang, and Suk Bong Choi. 2023. "Coaching Leadership and Creative Performance: A Serial Mediation Model of Psychological Empowerment and Constructive Voice Behavior." *Frontiers in Psychology* 14 (14). https://doi.org/10.3389/fpsyg.2023.1077594

"HubSpot Careers." 2025. HubSpot.com. https://www.hubspot.com/culture

In-N-Out. 2020. "Food Quality." In-n-Out.com. https://www.in-n-out.com/menu/food-quality

In-N-Out.com. 2020. https://www.in-n-out.com/mediakit/

Isaac, Mike. "Uber's C.E.O. Plays with Fire." *The New York Times*, April 23, 2017.

https://www.nytimes.com/2017/04/23/technology/travis-kalanick-pushes-uber-and-himself-to-the-precipice.html

Johnson, Greg. "Trader Joe's: A Different Culture." Blue Book. March 19, 2021. https://www.bluebookservices.com/trader-joes-a-different-culture

"Key Concepts from Employees First, Customers Second." HCL Tech. 2022. https://www.hcltech.com/sites/default/files/documents/resources/brochure/files/emplyeesfirstminibook.pdf

Klotz, Damon. 2024. "Culture First." Podcast. Culture Amp. https://www.cultureamp.com/podcast/patagonia

Knauth, Dietrich and Brendan Pierson. "FTX's New CEO Helped Bolster Enron Victims' Recovery." *Reuters*, November 15, 2022. https://www.reuters.com/technology/ftxs-new-ceo-helped-bolster-enron-victims-recovery-2022-11-15/

Kolhatkar, Sheelah. "At Uber, a New C.E.O. Shifts Gears." *The New Yorker*, March 30, 2018. https://www.newyorker.com/magazine/2018/04/09/at-uber-a-new-ceo-shifts-gears

Korn Ferry. "71% of U.S. CEOs Experience Imposter Syndrome, New Korn Ferry Research Finds." June 6, 2024. https://www.kornferry.com/about-us/press/71percent-of-us-ceos-experience-imposter-syndrome-new-korn-ferry-research-finds

Kosoff, Maya. "Uber Hires an Obama Alum to Save It from Another P.R. Disaster." *Vanity Fair*, February 21, 2017. https://www.vanityfair.com/news/2017/02/uber-hires-an-obama-alum-to-save-it-from-another-pr-disaster

Laker, Benjamin. "Culture Is a Company's Single Most Powerful Advantage. Here's Why." *Forbes*, December 10, 2021. https://www.forbes.com/sites/benjaminlaker/2021/04/23/

culture-is-a-companys-single-most-powerful-advantage-heres-why/

Lencioni, Patrick. 2002. *The Five Dysfunctions of a Team: A Leadership Fable*. Jossey-Bass.

Lewis, Charles. "The Enron Collapse – A Financial Scandal Rooted in Politics." Center for Public Integrity. February 25, 2002. https://publicintegrity.org/inequality-poverty-opportunity/commentary-the-enron-collapse-a-financial-scandal-rooted-in-politics/

Lynch, Brooke. "Why Chick-Fil-A Employees Deliver Outstanding Customer Service | CCW Digital." CCW Digital. November 21, 2024. https://www.customercontactweekdigital.com/ccw-analyst-insights/articles/chick-fil-a-employee-experience

Mashayekhi, Rey. "The Remarkable Rise—and Epic Fall—of WeWork's Charismatic Controversial Founder Adam Neumann." *Fortune*, September 25, 2019. https://fortune.com/2019/09/25/the-remarkable-rise-and-epic-fall-of-weworks-charismatic-controversial-founder-adam-neumann/

McDonald's Corporation. "Hamburger University – Our Signature Learning Approach." McDonalds.com. https://corporate.mcdonalds.com/corpmcd/our-people/training-and-education/hamburger-university.html

Nayar, Vineet. 2010. *Employees First, Customers Second: Turning Conventional Management Upside Down*. Harvard Business Review Press.

Nayar, Vineet. "Put Your Employees First." *Harvard Business Review*, July 20, 2010. https://hbr.org/2010/07/put-your-employees-first

"Our Story." Salesforce. 2022. https://www.salesforce.com/company/careers/culture

"Our Values Guide Every Decision." Salesforce. 2022. https://www.salesforce.com/company/our-values

Owens, Bradley P., and David R. Hekman. 2016. "How Does Leader Humility Influence Team Performance? Exploring the Mechanisms of Contagion and Collective Promotion Focus." *Academy of Management Journal* 59 (3): 1088–1111. https://doi.org/10.5465/amj.2013.0660

Packard, David. 1995. *The HP Way*. HarperBusiness.

Panayides, Jasmine. "How to Measure the ROI of Positive Company Culture." MyHRFuture. March 13, 2024. https://www.myhrfuture.com/blog/2024/3/13/how-to-measure-the-roi-of-positive-company-culture

Patagonia Employee Benefits. "Empowering Through Activism and Civic Engagement." 2025. https://careers.patagonia.com/us/en/benefit

Perman, Cindy. "Costco and Other Retailers Prove a 'Good Jobs' Strategy Works." Harvard Business School. December 3, 2024. https://www.hbs.edu/bigs/costco-and-other-retailers-prove-a-good-jobs-strategy-work

Petrak, Lynn. "Yes, Being Nice Is a Thing at Trader Joe's." Progressive Grocer. August 9, 2024. https://progressivegrocer.com/yes-being-nice-thing-trader-joes

Phelan, Matt. "Recognition (Acknowledgement)." The Happiness Index. September 12, 2022, https://thehappinessindex.com/blog/neuroscience-recognition/

PwC. "PwC Innovation Benchmark 2023." 2023. https://www.pwc.com/gr/en/publications/specific-to-all-industries-index/innovation-benchmark-report.html?utm_source=chatgpt.com

REI. "REI Co-Op Continues Its Annual Black Friday Tradition, Closing Its Doors and Paying Employees to Opt Outside." REI. October 2, 2024. https://www.rei.com/newsroom/article/rei-co-op-continues-its-annual-black-friday-tradition-closing-its-doors-and-paying-employees-to-opt-outside?msockid=371b6b8f6f3f6e1926f07d1d6e376f36

Reinhold, Diane and Tracy Patterson. "Leadership Development Research: What Works Best – and What Doesn't?" CCL. Center for Creative Leadership. November 30, 2021. https://www.ccl.org/articles/leading-effectively-articles/3-keys-making-leadership-development-work/

Relihan, Tom. "How Costco's Obsession with Culture Drove Success." MIT Sloan. May 11, 2018. https://mitsloan.mit.edu/ideas-made-to-matter/how-costcos-obsession-culture-drove-success

Renascence. 2024. "How the Ritz-Carlton Enhances Customer Experience (CX) Through Personalized Service and Luxury." Renascence.io. https://www.renascence.io/journal/how-the-ritz-carlton-enhances-customer-experience-cx-through-personalized-service-and-luxury

Robinson, David. "Remote Work vs. In-Person: What Does the Research Say?" Vertical Performance. March 6, 2023. https://verticalperformance.us/remote-work-vs-in-person-what-does-the-research-say/

Rockey, James C., Harriet M.J. Smith, and Heather D. Flowe. 2021. "Dirty Looks: Politicians' Appearance and Unethical Behaviour." *The Leadership Quarterly* 33 (1): 101561. https://doi.org/10.1016/j.leaqua.2021.101561

S, Athira V. "Patagonia Company Culture in Action: How HR Can Apply These Values Anywhere." CultureMonkey. July 24, 2025. https://www.culturemonkey.io/employee-engagement/patagonia-company-culture/

Sarmah, Pallavi, Anja Van den Broeck, Bert Schreurs, Karin Proost, and Filip Germeys. 2021. "Autonomy Supportive and Controlling Leadership as Antecedents of Work Design and Employee Well-Being." *BRQ Business Research Quarterly* 25(1): 234094442110545. https://doi.org/10.1177/23409444211054508

Semuels, Alana. "How CEO John Santora Is Helping WeWork Grow Up." *Time*, March 30, 2025. https://time.com/7272877/wework-ceo-john-santora-interview/

Sinek, Simon. 2009. *Start with Why: How Great Leaders Inspire Everyone to Take Action*. London: Penguin.

Smialek, Jeanna. "In-N-Out Burger's Secret Sauce for Success: Consistency and Culture." *Bloomberg*, September 5, 2022. https://www.bloomberg.com/news/articles/2022-09-05/in-n-out-burger-keeps-its-culture-and-quality-while-growing

Smiedt, David. "The Disney Hug Rule You Need to Know About." *Adelaidenow*, March 26, 2024. https://www.adelaidenow.com.au/lifestyle/the-disney-hug-rule-you-need-to-know-about/news-story/677a11fb7773d1d437e355c474ef6d3e?utm_source

Snyder, Lynsi. 2023. *The Ins-N-Outs of In-N-Out Burger*. Thomas Nelson.

Southwest Airlines. "Our People and Culture | Southwest Airlines." www.southwest.com. 2025. https://www.southwest.com/citizenship/people/

Sprout Social. "2023 Diversity, Equity & Inclusion Report." 2023. https://media.sproutsocial.com/uploads/Sprout-Social_2023-DEI-report.pdf

"State of Remote Work 2021 | Owl Labs." Owllabs.com. https://www.owllabs.com/state-of-remote-work/2021

Sweet, Ken. "Fed Lifts Restrictions Placed on Wells Fargo in 2018 Because of Its Fake-Accounts Scandal." *AP News*, June 3, 2025. https://apnews.com/article/e1d79548c0da446320c441e88d e3eea4

Swisher, K. "With Her Blog Post About Toxic Bro-Culture at Uber, Susan Fowler Proved That One Person Can Make a Difference." *Vox*, June 22, 2017. https://www.vox.com/2017/6/21/15844852/uber-toxic-bro-company-culture-susan-fowler-blog-post

Talent Strategies. September 12, 2023. https://www.titustalent.com/insights/zappos-a-case-study-into-company-culture

Taube, Aaron. "Why In-N-Out Burger Pays Managers $160,000 a Year." *Business Insider*, January 26, 2018. https://www.businessinsider.com/in-n-out-employee-pay-2018-1

The Guardian, Julia Carrie Wong, and Sam Morris. "Collision Course: Uber's Terrible 2017." AlterNet. December 27, 2017. https://www.alternet.org/2017/12/collision-course-ubers-terrible-2017

The Guardian and Matthew Zeitlin. "Why WeWork Went Wrong." Ventured. December 20, 2019. https://ourblog.siliconbaypartners.com/why-wework-went-wrong/

"The Remote Playbook." GitLab. 2023. https://learn.gitlab.com/allremote/remote-playbook

Thiha Tun, Zaw. "Theranos: A Fallen Unicorn." Investopedia. March 21, 2025. https://www.investopedia.com/articles/investing/020116/theranos-fallen-unicorn.asp

Time. "Wells Fargo Customer Fraud Deals Political Setback to Banks." *Time*, September 2016. https://time.com/4504031/wells-fargo-customer-fraud-deals-political-setback-to-banks/

Training Simplified. "The Secret Sauce Behind Chick-Fil-A's World-Class Service." Training Simplified. January 21, 2025. https://www.trainingsimplified.com/blog/the-secret-sauce-behind-chick-fil-as-world-class-service

Triplett, Angela. "4 Lessons in Employee Empowerment Courtesy of Chick-Fil-A." Customer Service Profiles LLC. November 2, 2016. https://www.csp.com/chick-fil-a

University of Oxford. "Happy Workers Are 13% More Productive." University of Oxford. October 24, 2019. https://www.ox.ac.uk/news/2019-10-24-happy-workers-are-13-more-productive

Weiss, Howard M. and Russell Cropanzano. 1996. "Affective Events Theory: A Theoretical Discussion of the Structure, Causes and Consequences of Affective Experiences at Work." *Research in Organizational Behavior* 18, 1–74. https://psycnet.apa.org/record/1996-98665-001

"What Makes Zappos a Leader in Customer Experience (CX)?" 2023. Renascence.io. https://www.renascence.io/journal/what-makes-zappos-a-leader-in-customer-experience-cx

Whitehead-Smith, Elle. "Flexibility Is for Life – Not Just the World Cup." The Happiness Index. November 22, 2022, https://thehappinessindex.com/blog/flexibility-world-cup/

Whitehead-Smith, Elle. "Gallup's State of the Global Workplace Report Summary." Thehappinessindex.com. July 10, 2024. https://thehappinessindex.com/blog/gallup-global-workplace-report/

Wigert, Ben, Sangeeta Agrawal, Kristin Barry, and Ellyn Maese. "The Wellbeing-Engagement Paradox of 2020." Gallup. March 13, 2021. https://www.gallup.com/workplace/336941/employee-engagement-meta-analysis.aspx

Wired. "A Look Inside Theranos' Dysfunctional Corporate Culture." *Wired*, May 21, 2018.

Wuchty, Stefan, and Brian Uzzi. 2015. "Diversity and Creativity in Science and Engineering." *PNAS* (112), 35. https://www.researchgate.net/publication/363080733_Gender-diverse_teams_produce_more_novel_and_higher-impact_scientific_ideas

"Work Trend Index: Microsoft's Latest Research on the Ways We Work." Microsoft.com. March 8, 2023. https://www.microsoft.com/en-us/worklab/work-trend-index?msockid=371b6b8f6f3f6e1926f07d1d6e376f36

"Workforce 2025: Power Shifts." Korn Ferry. July 18, 2025. https://www.kornferry.com/about-us/press/korn-ferry-hay-group-global-study-finds-employee-engagement-at-critically-low-levels

Yang, Liu-Qin, Russell Cropanzano, Catherine S Daus, and Vicente Martínez-Tur. 2020. *The Cambridge Handbook of Workplace Affect*. Cambridge University Press. https://www.cambridge.org/core/books/cambridge-handbook-of-workplace-affect/EBFED416C157F1ECCD0CEE3ED69DCE5B

Let's Keep the Conversation Going.

Leadership doesn't end on the last page; it starts with what you do next.

Download your free copy of The Culture Checklist!

ACCESS MORE LEADERSHIP TOOLS

Visit NoEGOpolicy.com to get your exclusive download and start building a culture that endures.

www.ingramcontent.com/pod-product-compliance
Lightning Source LLC
Chambersburg PA
CBHW022113210326
41597CB00047B/294